STORY OF THE MOVIE

ORCHARD BOOKS

First published in Great Britain in 2023 by Hodder & Stoughton

1 3 5 7 9 10 8 6 4 2

DreamWorks Trolls Band Together © DreamWorks Animation LLC, 2023
All Rights Reserved.

A CIP catalogue record for this book is available from the British Library

ISBN 978 1 408 37052 0

Printed and bound in Great Britain by Clays Ltd, Elcograf S.p.A.

The paper and board used in this book are made from wood from
responsible sources.

Orchard Books
An imprint of Hachette Children's Group
50 Victoria Embankment
London EC4Y 0DZ
An Hachette UK Company
www.hachette.co.uk
www.hachettechildrens.co.uk

STORY OF THE MOVIE

ORCHARD

CHAPTER ONE

This story began a bunch of years ago, before
the Bergens discovered they loved eating Trolls.
Before the Trolls escaped from the Bergens.
And before Poppy and Branch taught the
Bergens they could be happy without eating
Trolls. Before all that stuff happened, there was
a band of boy Trolls.

A band called BroZone.

BroZone was popular. SUPER popular.
Trolls flocked to their live concerts. Collected
their albums. Lined up to get their autographs.
Memorised the lyrics to their hit songs.
Everyone loved their catchy tunes, their tight
harmonies, their smooth dance moves. Trolls
just couldn't get enough of BroZone!

On the day this story begins, the five

members of BroZone (who also happened to be brothers) were about to kick off their Perfect Family Harmony Tour with a huge concert in the old Troll Tree's arena. "BROZONE! BROZONE! BROZONE!" the massive crowd chanted, eager to see their favourite performers live onstage.

"Three minutes to showtime!" the stage manager announced.

A blue-haired baby Troll in a nappy – the youngest brother – nervously peeked out through the stage curtain. John Dory, the oldest brother, paced behind him, going over the list of songs they'd sing that day, trying to pick the best order possible.

"All right, guys," said John Dory, pulling a pen out of his green hair. "We're gonna open with 'Girl Baby Girl' and close with 'Baby Baby Girl'. Wait, no – that doesn't sound right. Oh, I got it! Open with 'Baby Baby Girl' and close with 'Baby Baby Girl Woman'. Yes! We are going to make boy-band history tonight." He looked around. "Where are my brothers?" He hurried back into the dressing room to make sure they were all ready to go onstage.

Spruce, the heartthrob brother with purple hair, was doing sit-ups. Clay, the funny brother with yellow hair, walked up to John Dory wearing a sparkly pair of underpants.

"Do I really have to keep wearing these things?" he complained.

"C'mon, Clay," John Dory said. "They're 'Funderdrawers'! Underwear, but seventy-six per cent more fun! Now let's see those dance moves!"

"Fine," Clay said with a sigh. He did a quick series of dance steps, naming them while executing them perfectly. "Rusty robot into wiggle worm, and end on caliente puppet."

"Not bad," John Dory said, stroking his chin. "But your robot could be rustier. And your worm wigglier."

Clay looked annoyed. "Don't you want my

puppet caliente-er?"

"I wasn't going to say it," John Dory said, "but yeah. Definitely."

Floyd, the shy, sensitive brother, put the finishing touches on his magenta hair. "Bro," he told John Dory, "you look stressed. Breathe."

"Of course I'm stressed!" John Dory said, exasperated. "It's the first show of the tour. We have to hit the Perfect Family Harmony. We promised the fans!"

Floyd patted the air with both hands. "Calm down," he whispered. "You're making Baby Branch nervous." Baby Branch was the youngest brother in BroZone, who would grow up to be the Troll known simply as Branch. Back then, he was known to the fans as 'The Baby'.

John Dory looked over at Baby Branch, who was anxiously fiddling with the pink glasses he'd been given to wear onstage. "He's not allowed to be nervous," John Dory said sternly.

"He's got to be perfect!"

Floyd shook his head. "Cut him some slack, John Dory. It's his first live show." He went over to his youngest brother and bent down. "Hey, Baby Branch. How you feelin'?"

Baby Branch clutched his stomach. "Like I'm gonna barf and pass out."

"You got the preshow jitters," Floyd said, patting him reassuringly. "It's totally normal. Everyone gets them. Know what I do when I get them?"

"Barf and pass out?" Baby Branch guessed.

Floyd chuckled. "I remember that I'm with my brothers, and that when we come together, there's nothing we can't do."

Clapping his hands, John Dory called his brothers to gather around. As the oldest, he'd long since taken the role of leader. "All right, boys," he lectured. "Just remember: no matter what you do, follow my lead."

From out in the arena, they could hear

the restless audience chanting, "PER-FECT! FA-MI-LY! HAR-MO-NY! PER-FECT! FA-MI-LY! HAR-MO-NY!!"

Clay gulped. "It's just so much pressure!"

The stage manager poked his head into the dressing room. "Ten seconds!"

"If we can't hit the Perfect Family Harmony, we aren't perfect," John Dory insisted. "And if we aren't perfect, we're NOTHING! Being nothing is definitely not an option. So just follow my lead." He stuck his hand out, palm down. "Let's do this!"

Each of his brothers piled their hands on top of his. Together, John Dory, Spruce, Clay, Floyd and Baby Branch shouted, "IT'S BRO TIME!"

CHAPTER TWO

A smooth-voiced announcer spoke through the arena's loudspeakers. "Ladies and gentlemen! Here they are!" Throngs of fans cheered, clapped and stomped their feet.

"The Heartthrob!" the announcer said, introducing Spruce. Spruce walked onstage blowing kisses. Pop Trolls fans squealed with delight. Spruce was so dreamy!

"The Fun Boy!" said the announcer, and Clay popped out through the curtains doing his dance moves. The audience laughed and applauded. They thought he was hilarious, no matter what he did.

"The Sensitive One!" Floyd entered slowly with both hands pressed against his heart. The Trolls closest to the stage sighed, wishing they could take care of him and protect him from all the harsh things in the world.

"The Leader!" said the announcer. John Dory strode onstage, full of confidence and determination. The audience cheered, ready to follow him wherever he wanted to take them.

"And making his first live appearance, The Baby!" Glitter burst over the stage, revealing Branch suspended on a wire.

"Awwww!" the whole audience said, charmed by the adorable sight.

BroZone rolled right into their first song. Cool, calm and collected, John Dory danced up a storm. Spruce blew another kiss, and the fans went wild. Clay added little goofy touches to the dance steps, getting lots of laughs. Floyd shed a single tear as he sang. And Branch flipped down off his wire, sticking the landing perfectly, nailing every move and every note as the five brothers came together.

They were in perfect sync, moving and

singing as if they were one person. Everyone in the audience sensed that something very special was happening on the stage that night. They felt lucky to be there to witness it.

The five brothers hit a chord and held it. Offstage, a water glass broke. *KSHHH!* Overhead, a light bulb shattered. *SHHINK!* The brothers looked at each other. It was happening! They were achieving the PERFECT FAMILY HARMONY!

"It's working!" John Dory hissed. "Come on, guys! Follow my lead!"

But when they realised how close they were to perfection, the brothers got excited and tried way too hard, pushing their singing till it was out of tune. Their harmonies were off. They messed up the rhythms. And then their moves went out of whack. They bumped into each other, they tripped, they got tangled up in a vine and swung into the air, banging into each other and finally bringing the whole set down. *CRASH!*

Stunned, the audience went silent.

The stage manager crept into view. "Ladies and gentlemen," he said to the crowd, "please stand by. We are experiencing" – he looked around, unsure how to describe the disaster that had just taken place – "some stuff," he concluded.

Moments later, the members of BroZone stormed into their dressing room. "See what happens when you don't follow my lead?" John Dory said accusingly.

"Dude!" Spruce said sharply. "That is EXACTLY what happens when we follow your lead!"

Branch looked up at his older brothers anxiously. He didn't like it when they fought.

"Oh, so this whole mess is MY fault?" John Dory asked. "Is that what you're saying? I know we can reach the Perfect Family Harmony—"

"What if we don't want to?" Spruce interrupted.

Clay stepped next to Spruce. "Yeah, dude. BroZone used to be about fun. Now it's all about being perfect."

John Dory winced. That stung.

"You know what?" Spruce said, suddenly making up his mind. "I'm done playing the heartthrob. My exquisitely chiselled rock-hard abs and I quit!"

"I quit too," Clay said. "And you can keep these!" He tossed the sparkly Funderdrawers right in John Dory's face. "I'm more than just the fun one. I'm in a sad-book club! I'm gonna go find Trolls who take me seriously."

"Fine!" John Dory shouted, tossing the Funderdrawers on the floor. "I don't need this. I'm out too. I'm done. I'm gonna go hike the Neverglade Trail. By myself. Bro-lone. Yeah, that's right. Bro-bro goin' solo!"

He grabbed his backpack and climbing gear and swung his leg over the sill of the dressing room window, ready to rappel down to the ground. "Goodbye forever!"

"Fine by me!" Clay said, stomping out of the room.

"Good riddance!" Spruce said as he exited.

"Guys!" Floyd called after them in his gentle voice. "Please, guys! Come on!" But his pleas were too late. John Dory, Clay and Spruce were gone.

Branch looked like he was going to cry. "It's my fault," he said. "I ruined everything."

Floyd crouched down and put a comforting hand on his baby brother's shoulder. "Branch, this is not your fault." He stood up and turned to go.

"Floyd!" Branch protested. "You're not leaving too?"

Floyd turned back and smiled gently. "Not forever. I'll be back, I promise. But right now, I have to follow my heart. It's telling me it's time to start a solo career."

Branch looked stricken. "But what am I gonna do?" he said, his voice breaking.

"Branch, you're going to do the most important thing of all," Floyd assured him. "You're going to take care of Grandma."

Their grandmother sat at a table in the dressing room, dealing cards. "Come on, Branch," she urged. "Let's play some rummy! But I won't let you win because I play for the money."

"When you miss me," Floyd said, "you can wear this." He took off his green waistcoat and handed it to Branch. "It'll be like I'm right here with you."

Baby Branch ran to his dressing-room mirror and grabbed a drawing he'd made. He handed it to Floyd. "And when you come back, we'll make our hideout."

Studying the drawing of a hideout with rooms for each brother, Floyd smiled. It had a kitchen, a lounge and special cupboards for all their costumes. "Definitely. Is that a ten-storey waterslide?"

Branch nodded proudly. "Yeah, that's how we shower."

"Well, then, we'd better put this plan in a safe place," Floyd said, folding up the drawing and putting it in the inner pocket of the waistcoat he'd just given Branch. He hugged his brother and said, "I'll see you soon, Baby Branch."

He walked to the door, turned to his brother and waved goodbye.

"Bye," Branch said, waving back. "See you later."

CHAPTER THREE

A bunch of years later, grown-up Branch was listening to an old BroZone album in Grandma's tree pod. Grandma was long gone, eaten by a Bergen. Branch hadn't seen his brothers once in all those years since BroZone had broken up. Listening to his younger self and his brothers sing together, he smiled. Tears formed in his eyes.

Poppy peeked through the door, watching Branch for a moment. Then she cleared her throat to let him know she was there and said, "Branch?"

He quickly stopped the music and tossed the album aside. "What? Oh! Hey."

Poppy walked into the pod. "Are you all right? You're smiling and crying at the same time, and it kinda looks like it's hurting your face."

"It does hurt my face," Branch admitted. "I guess I'm just missing my—" He was about to say 'brothers', but quickly stopped himself, remembering that he'd never told Poppy about his four brothers. ". . . grandma. I was just listening to some of her old records."

Poppy picked up the album he'd tossed aside. "BroZone? No way! I LOVE BroZone!"

"Really?" Branch said, surprised and pleased. Then he put on a bored voice, pretending he couldn't believe Poppy loved such an uncool band. "I mean, really?"

"I didn't know you liked them too," Poppy said, excited.

Branch scowled and shook his head. "I don't. I'm actually hate-listening. It's a new thing. My grandma had very questionable taste." He gestured towards the room they were standing in, hoping to change the subject. "I mean, just look at how she decorated this place. I'm sorry, but there are just some things that shouldn't be macramé'd. Am I right?"

He quickly tucked the album back in with the others, making sure Poppy couldn't see the picture of him as a baby on the cover.

Poppy narrowed her gaze suspiciously. "It kinda seems like there's something you're not telling me."

"What? Don't be silly. No . . ."

"Hey, I need you to be real with me," Poppy said firmly. "It seems like more than a macramé issue. If you're having feelings, you can talk about them with me."

"OK, you're right." Branch checked his watch. "Oh, hey! Look at the time. We're going to be late to the royal wedding! Let's go get married!"

Poppy looked shocked. "Branch!"

"What?" Branch looked a little stunned too. "I mean, let's get Bridget and Gristle married."

"Yeah," Poppy said. "Because it would be weird if we got married."

"So weird," Branch agreed. "Duh."

"Wow, the weirdest," Poppy said. "It's, like, weird that we're still talking about how weird it was, and it's, like, fifteen seconds later."

"Bleh," Branch said, shaking his shoulders as though he were trying to shake off the weirdness of the moment.

"Bleh!" Poppy said a little too loudly.

The two Trolls were already dressed for the wedding. Poppy wore a dress with a puffy white skirt that looked like a cloud, and a coloured headband decorated with puffballs. Branch was decked out in a shiny green-and-blue waistcoat, gleaming trousers and a purple bow tie. They ran out of the pod, jumped on the backs of two light-blue Glowflies and zipped off to the royal wedding of King Gristle and his beautiful bride, Bridget.

CHAPTER FOUR

Poppy and Branch flew straight to Bergen Town, where preparations were already well underway for the royal wedding. The streets were crowded with Bergens and Trolls who were excited for the ceremony and the big party afterwards. Working together, they hung decorations, set up chairs and covered tables with food. Many were already singing and dancing.

Up at the castle, Gristle awoke in his bedroom. "Oh boy," he said, rubbing his head. "That was a crazy bachelor party!"

Cloud Guy woke up in the castle too, having spent the night. "Uhh," he groaned. "Cloud Guy don't feel so good." He'd had way too much to eat at the party, where he'd stuffed himself silly.

Branch, Cooper and Prince D helped Gristle get cleaned up and dressed in a tuxedo, so he'd look his best on his wedding day.

Poppy went straight to Bridget's room to help style her hair and get her dressed. "Now let's get this dress right," Poppy said.

Satin and Chenille, the Troll twin sisters who excelled in all things fashion-related, dressed Bridget in a fancy gown they'd made themselves. It was frilly and lacy, with a long skirt and puffy sleeves.

Poppy studied it carefully. "Uh, no," she declared. It just wasn't Bridget's style.

Undiscouraged, Satin and Chenille popped another dress over Bridget's head. They'd brought plenty of options, and this one featured different colours. But Poppy still wasn't satisfied.

"Uh-uh," she said, shaking her head. "Nope. Next."

The twins kept trying more dresses until

Poppy spotted a Bergen walking by outside
carrying a big bunch of colourful balloons. It
gave Poppy an idea for a fabulous dress. "Satin!
Chenille!" she cried, pointing out the window.

They got Poppy's idea right away.

"Fashion . . ." Satin began.

". . . emergency!" Chenille said, completing
her sister's thought as they swung into action.

Near the town square, where the wedding
ceremony would soon take place, Guy
Diamond sat on a bench with his son, Tiny
Diamond. The little Troll looked absolutely
adorable in a colourful flower costume with big
petals around his face.

But he hated it.

"Look at you, Tiny Diamond!" his dad
gushed in his techno voice. "You make the cu-U-
U-test little flo-OW-er bo-OO-y!"

Tiny Diamond scowled. "Oh, come on,

Daddy!" he groaned. "I'm not a baby any
more! I'm the cutest little flower MAN!" He
ripped the costume off.

"But, Tiny," Guy Diamond pointed out,
"you're only a month old!"

Poppy flew in on a bunch of balloons and
landed next to them. "Come on, guys!" she
urged. "It's time!"

"Ooooh, balloons!" Tiny Diamond cooed.

They hurried to their places. Bridget floated
down in a dress made from gold balloons,
landing right on the long carpet. At the other
end, Gristle waited on the terrace, his breath
taken away by his bride's beauty.

Poppy climbed up Bridget's balloon dress to
share one last moment with her friend before she
got married. "Bridget, you look so beautiful!"

"Thank you so much for being my maid of
honour," Bridget replied. "I couldn't have done
this without you."

"Oh, of course, Bridget!" Poppy said, adjusting

a stray lock of the Bergen's lavender hair. "I love you like a sister. Probably. I don't have a sister, so I wouldn't know. Which is fine. It's something I'm coming to terms with, slowly, but—"

Bridget held up a finger. "Uh, Poppy? Can we maybe unpack the sister thing *after* the wedding vows?"

Poppy blushed. "Of course! You go get him, girl! Before I do!" She popped one of the balloons on Bridget's dress. Then all the balloons popped, showering the square with gold glitter! Underneath the balloons, Bridget was wearing a white lace jumpsuit, a belt with a gold buckle, a veil, a little golden crown and roller skates – a tribute to her first date with Gristle. She slowly skated down the carpet and made her way up the steps – a little awkwardly, thanks to the roller skates.

Tears of joy streaked down Gristle's face as he beheld his bride. "Like a beautiful angel, sent from heaven . . ."

Gristle's Aunt Smead, a tall Bergen with goggles and hair that stood straight up, was in charge of leading the happy couple through their wedding vows. She leaned over and joked, "Hey, Bridget, you still have time to run for it!"

"Ha, ha – very funny, Aunt Smead," Gristle said. Along with his powder-blue tux, he was sporting his usual spotted-fur cape with a green bejewelled clasp, his crown and white shoes with black socks. Stylin'!

Smiling, Aunt Smead launched right into the ceremony, addressing the crowd of happy Trolls and Bergens. "Dearly beloved," she began, "we are gathered here today to celebrate the sweet, sweet love of Bridget . . ." She turned to the bride. "Hey, girl!" Then she nodded towards her nephew. "And Mister Yummy-Yummy Tummy himself, King Gristle! Now, falling in love is easy. We've all done it. I've done it hundreds of times. But marriage is—"

"STOP THE WEDDING!"

CHAPTER FIVE

The crowd gasped, shocked by the interruption.
A Troll leaped from a high tower right into
the middle of the wedding ceremony. He had
blueish-green hair, blue skin and a purple nose.
He wore a brown waistcoat trimmed with
spotted white fur and matching brown gloves.
Pushed up on his forehead, above his eyebrows,
was a pair of goggles with reflective magenta
glass set in green frames. He was a complete
stranger – none of the Bergens or Trolls
recognised him. Except for one.

Branch knew his big brother, John Dory, as
soon as he saw him, even after so many years.

"Sorry, is this bad timing?" John Dory asked.
He looked around the crowd of Trolls and
Bergens. "I'm just trying to find a Troll named ..."

He spotted Branch. "Ah! BABY BRANCH!"

Branch decided to pretend he had no idea who John Dory was. "You're making a mistake, stranger who looks similar to me. There's no Branch here."

But John Dory ignored this. Taking Branch by the shoulders, he said, "Look at you! You got so big! You're not a branch any more – you're more like a trunk! Junk in the trunk! But I bet I can still pick you up. C'mon!" He picked up his brother, despite his yelps of protest. "Oooh, you got heavy!" John Dory grunted. "There goes my back!"

Poppy stepped up to confront the stranger. "Hey, stop right there!" she told him. "You put my boyfriend down and tell us who you are and what you want!"

THUD. John Dory dropped Branch.

"Ow!" Branch cried.

"Hey, whoa now!" John Dory exclaimed. "You're right. Totally rude of me. Didn't introduce myself. I'm Branch's brother."

"*WHAT?*" Poppy gasped, astonished at this news.

The whole crowd gasped too. "Ooooh, drama!" Tiny Diamond squealed, delighted. "Corn me, Dinkles!"

Mr Dinkles, Biggie's pet worm, obliged, providing Tiny Diamond with a tub of tasty popcorn. Tiny Diamond munched on the snack, eagerly watching to see what would happen next.

"Correction," Branch said, getting to his feet. "*Used* to be my brother. Not any more."

Poppy pulled Branch aside. "Hey, uh, remember earlier, when I said you should open up to me and be real?"

"Well—" Branch started to say.

"YOU COULD HAVE STARTED BY TELLING ME YOU HAD A SECRET BROTHER!" Poppy shouted.

"*Former* brother," Branch corrected.

"THAT'S NOT HOW DNA WORKS!" Poppy insisted. She turned to her father, King Peppy. "Dad, did you know about this?"

King Peppy looked nervous, his eyes darting about. "What would I know about secret family members?"

Poppy rushed over and introduced herself to John Dory. "Oh my gosh, I was being so rude! I've never met anyone from Branch's family before. I'm Poppy. Branch's girlfriend. Should we hug? Fist-bump? Smile and wave for now and see where the night takes us?"

"All of the above!" John Dory said, hugging Poppy, bumping her fist with his, and waving and smiling.

Suddenly Poppy recognised him. "Wait, I know you! You're the guy from BroZone! We were just listening to them."

All around, Trolls gasped in amazement, chattering to each other excitedly.

"A member of BroZone! Here!"

"Branch's brother!"

"*Whaaaaaat*!"

Poppy could barely contain her excitement. "Oh, wait, wait, wait! Don't tell me! Um, well, you're not The Heartthrob . . ."

"That's *your* opinion," John Dory said.

"The Fun One, right?" Poppy guessed. "No, you're kind of uptight . . ."

"Uptight?"

"Not the Sensitive One, either . . ."

"OK, a lot of assumptions for someone you just met thirty seconds ago."

"Oooh! Ooooh! I've got it! You're John Dory . . ." she began.

"The leader," John Dory finished proudly.

". . . the old one!" Poppy said.

John Dory rolled his eyes. King Gristle spoke up. "Sorry to interrupt, but we lose the venue at eleven, so—"

"Shh, I'm trying to listen," Bridget said, shushing him. "Very hot gossip!"

"So, if you're Branch's bro," Poppy said, putting it all together, "that means all the other BroZone bros are Branch's bros too!" She whirled on her boyfriend. "BRANCH! How come you never told me?"

Branch looked uncomfortable. "Because it's . . . complicated."

Poppy patted his arm reassuringly. "Ohhhh, sweetie. I understand. You never told me because you weren't in the band."

"Oh, Branch was in the band, all right," John Dory said.

CHAPTER SIX

If Poppy had been shocked when she learned
Branch had a brother, that was nothing
compared to how shocked she was to learn he'd
been in her favourite band of all time. "WHAT?!"
she exclaimed. "No way! Which one was he?"

"The Baby," John Dory answered.

"The Baby? No, that's impossible," Poppy
argued. "The Baby had glasses."

"Oh, and a nappy," John Dory added. "Let's
not forget the nappy."

"And a falsetto made of gold – not that
anyone cared," Branch snapped. "But that's
all in the past. Because they stopped being my
brothers the day they walked out on me and
never came back."

John Dory held up both hands. "Whoa, whoa,

whoa. That's not fair, Branch. I did come back, but no one was there. It wasn't until I heard about you saving the world from the 'rock apocalypse' that I realised you were even still alive." He was referring to when Branch and Poppy had stopped Queen Barb of the Rocker Trolls from turning all Trolls into rock zombies.

Branch rolled his eyes. "Oh, that's so sweet," he said sarcastically. "He realised I was still alive . . . twenty years too late!"

Leaning in, Poppy spoke directly to John Dory. "Sorry, he gets hangry if he skips breakfast."

"I *had* breakfast," Branch stated. "It was an avocado on toast with a poached egg, and it was delicious!"

Poppy took Branch aside. Lowering her voice, she said, "Branch, what's going on with you?"

"The question we should be asking is what's going on with *him*," he whispered angrily, jerking his thumb back towards John Dory. "I bet you he's only here because he needs something."

"That's not true," Poppy disagreed. "He's your brother!"

John Dory interrupted their conference. "Branch, I'm gonna be straight with you: I need something."

Branch knew it. "And there it is." He started to walk away.

"Wait, wait!" John Dory implored. "Hold up, Branch! It's about Floyd."

At the mention of his favourite brother, Branch stopped in his tracks. He turned to face John Dory, concerned. "Floyd? What do you mean?"

"He's in danger, man," John Dory said seriously. He told them about how he'd been out in the middle of nowhere, living alone in a van parked in the woods. "I hadn't heard from Floyd since the band broke up. Until I got a letter from him."

He pulled a wrinkled envelope out of his pocket to show them. It was addressed to "John Dory, Middle of Nowhere". He handed the letter to Branch to read out loud.

"'Dear John Dory,'" read Branch. "'I am being held against my will by superstars Velvet and Veneer. Come to Mount Rageous at once and bring our brothers. Love, Floyd.'" Branch looked up at John Dory.

"I didn't know where any of you were, so I went to Mount Rageous alone," John Dory said. Mount Rageous was a bright, shiny, colourful city full of concert halls and auditoriums where Mount Rageons could see all the latest celebrity performers. The pop singers mentioned in Floyd's note, Velvet and Veneer, performed in a big theatre there. Velvet was a young woman and Veneer was her brother.

When he got to the city of Mount Rageous, John Dory quickly found the theatre where Velvet and Veneer were performing. After making his way up to the roof and down through some air vents, he found the pop duo's dressing room.

"And there was Floyd," John Dory told Branch and Poppy.

CHAPTER SEVEN

The gentle Troll with the shock of magenta hair falling across one eye was trapped in a crystal bottle that had been cut from a single large diamond. The bottle was pulling Floyd's talent out of him and changing it into a perfume. There was a golden squeeze bulb attached to the bottle, so Velvet and Veneer could spray Floyd's Troll talent on to their vocal cords and sing like angels.

John Dory dropped down from the ceiling vent on a rope and landed face first next to Floyd's perfume bottle. *WHUMP!*

He lifted his head. "Yo, Floyd!"

"John Dory!" Floyd cried. "I can't believe it. I never thought I'd see any of my brothers again." He pressed his hands against the inside of the diamond bottle, and John Dory pressed his against the outside. It was the closest they could come to a reunion hug.

"I'm going to get you out of here, bro," John Dory promised.

Floyd looked frightened. "No, John Dory, *you've* gotta get out of here! You don't understand! Velvet and Veneer don't have any talent, so they've been stealing mine. They'll be back any minute for more."

"WHAT!" John Dory shouted, outraged that someone would steal someone else's talent. "That's even worse than lip-syncing!" He took a deep breath and squared his shoulders. "Not my brother. Not today." He tried to remove the bottle's stopper, but it was sealed tight. Grabbing whatever tools he could find in the dressing room, he tried to smash the bottle open, but nothing so much as cracked the hard surface.

"John, stop!" Floyd told him. "You're not

getting through. For that, we'd need something that can shatter diamonds."

"Of course," John Dory said, snapping his fingers. "The Perfect Family Harmony!"

Velvet's approaching voice came from the hall. "We're dying out there. Our voices sound like garbage! What we need is more Troll talent."

The evil sister and brother were coming.

"Run, John Dory!" Floyd begged. "Save yourself!"

Seeing no other option in the moment, as he couldn't sing the Perfect Family Harmony without his brothers, John Dory shot a grappling hook towards the ceiling and swung back up into the vents. But before he left, he promised, "Don't worry, Floyd! I'll be back with the bros! You have my word!"

In Bergen Town's main square, all the Trolls and Bergens had given John Dory's story their rapt attention, hanging on his every word. They were all silent for a moment, thinking about poor Floyd trapped in a diamond perfume bottle.

Then Poppy broke the spell. "So you came here to get the band back together and sing the Perfect Family Harmony?"

"Yeah," John Dory affirmed.

Branch made a sceptical face. "Oh, yeah," he said sarcastically. "So we can attempt to sing something we've only tried once and failed so miserably at that we broke up and never talked to each other again."

"We are SO in!" Poppy said enthusiastically.

"What!" Branch said. He couldn't believe Poppy was going along with this impossible plan. He turned to John Dory. "Uh, could you give us a second?" Pulling Poppy aside, Branch asked her, "OK, what are you doing?"

To Poppy, it was simple. "This is your second chance with your brothers, Branch."

Branch looked exasperated. "It's not that

easy, OK? You don't get it. You don't have any siblings."

"That's my point," Poppy countered. "Branch, you are so lucky to have a brother to fight for. I mean, if I had a sister . . ."

Overhearing his daughter, King Peppy looked nervous again, his eyes shifting back and forth, as though he suddenly didn't know where to look.

". . . we'd be best friends," Poppy continued, not noticing her dad's strange reaction. "We'd teach each other things, and we'd never fight . . ."

"Poppy," Branch interrupted, trying to stop her speech about the joys of sisterhood, which he'd heard before.

". . . and we'd always have each other's backs, and we wouldn't even have to talk because we'd think all the same thoughts . . ."

"Poppy," Branch said, trying again.

". . . and everyone would always ask if we

were twins, and we'd laugh and be like, 'Well, not technically, but . . .'"

"Poppy!" Branch said more firmly.

". . . but if she were ever in trouble, I would do everything I could to help her. I would show up—"

"OK, listen," Branch said, taking Poppy's shoulders in his hands. "If there was a brother I might do this for – and I'm not saying there is – it would be Floyd." He looked down at his waistcoat, remembering the day all those years ago when his sensitive brother had given it to him.

Poppy grinned. "I'm not hearing 'No!' Yeah! Woo!"

"Yes!" John Dory said, having overheard Branch. "Works for me!"

"BroZone 2.0!" Poppy said, instantly coming up with names for this adventure. "BroZone Reunion! BroZone: Here We Bro Again! BroZone: Where'd They Bro? I don't know, but we're gonna find them!"

CRRRACK! The ground opened up and an armadillo-like van broke through and drove to the surface! She had a tail, four green feet, two green eyes and a long red tongue. All the Trolls gaped, amazed at the sight.

"Ha!" John Dory laughed. "Looks like our ride has arrived! Here she is!"

King Gristle stared at the broken pavement. "Ohhh, that's coming out of the deposit."

CHAPTER EIGHT

It was the same van John Dory had been living in out in the middle of nowhere, before he received the letter from Floyd.

"Meet Rhonda, y'all," he said proudly. "Ain't she a beaut?"

Rhonda let out a massive roar and licked Poppy's entire body in one big swipe. *SHHHLURP!*

"She's, uh, really something," Branch said, at a loss for words to describe the bizarre creature.

"Um, I guess she likes me?" Poppy said, wiping off Rhonda's drool.

John Dory nodded. "Yes, she does. Or she's marking you as prey. You can never quite tell with Rhonda."

King Gristle and Bridget had been waiting

patiently through the entire exchange with John Dory, but now it was time to get on with their wedding.

"Uh, guys, if you don't mind," said Gristle, "I really cannot wait another minute to marry this gorgeous specimen."

Taking her cue, Aunt Smead quickly said in a loud voice, "I now pronounce you husband and wife!" Bridget pounced on Gristle, joyfully kissing her new spouse.

John Dory gestured towards Rhonda. "OK, all aboard who's going aboard!"

"Bye, everybody!" Poppy sang out, waving. "We're getting the band back together!" Her Troll and Bergen friends all waved back.

"Bye, Poppy!"

"Goodbye!"

"See you later!"

To King Gristle and his new queen, Poppy said, "Have an awesome honeymoon!"

Bridget beamed. "Thanks, Poppy!"

"I love you guys!" Poppy said, heading into the van with Branch and John Dory, ready to head off on their quest to find Spruce and Clay, sing the Perfect Family Harmony and rescue Floyd from the nasty clutches of Velvet and Veneer.

In the dazzling city of Mount Rageous, a young entertainment reporter named Kid Ritz was hosting a show about pop music called *The Bop on Top*.

"Today, on a very special episode of *The Bop on Top*," he said in a breathless, excited voice, "we're talking to overnight superstars Velvet and Veneer!" The show broadcast a video of Velvet and Veneer performing in fancy costumes with fur coats, gigantic hats and gold sunglasses. They were both tall and incredibly thin, with big blue eyes and long, perfectly styled green hair.

In a television studio, the pop duo's put-upon assistant Crimp swept off a chair, making sure it was immaculate before one of her bosses sat on it. Crimp resembled the head of a straw broom, with green eyes, white glasses and a purple hair bow scrunching a bun of papery hair on top of her head. She was much shorter than Velvet and Veneer, but was still at least three times the size of the average Troll.

Ignoring their assistant, Velvet launched herself on to the chair, squashing Crimp. *FWUNK!* "So," Velvet said to Kid Ritz, "what do you wanna know? I'm an open book."

Veneer scooted another chair next to his sister's and sat down, ready to be interviewed. "Wide open. We're gaping novels!"

Kid Ritz had his first question ready. "Who are some of your biggest influences?"

"Honestly," Veneer answered, looking at his sister adoringly, "Vel's always been my inspiration."

Velvet thought about it. "My biggest inspiration ... I'd have to go with also me."

Nodding, Kid Ritz looked straight into the camera. "Well, one thing's for sure: after just two months on the scene, the superstar duo will receive the prestigious Lifer Award. Be sure to catch it this weekend at the Rage Dome!" He turned back to Velvet and Veneer. "I guess the only other thing we wanna know is . . . how did you guys become the biggest superstars Mount Rageous has ever known? What's your secret?"

Veneer stood up, panicking. "Secret? We don't have a secret! WHO SAID WE HAVE A SECRET!"

"What my calm, casual-sounding brother means," Velvet explained smoothly, "is it really just takes lots of hard work and loads of natural talent."

Veneer smiled, looking guilty.

Later, the brother and sister tried laying down a song in their recording studio, but their voices kept cracking. They sounded terrible.

"Ugh," Velvet grunted. "If we're going to get another number-one single any time soon, we're gonna need more Troll talent!"

"Not to mention if we're going to make it through our Rage Dome show," Veneer pointed out.

"If you say you're not going to mention it," Velvet snapped, "don't mention it!"

"Sorry," Veneer apologised meekly.

"Come on," Velvet commanded, heading out of the recording studio.

Moments later, they burst into their dressing room, where Crimp was guarding Floyd, who was still imprisoned in the diamond perfume bottle.

"Crimp!" Velvet shouted at their assistant. "What are you doing? Why are you always hovering!"

Crimp looked confused. "Um, I'm standing?"

"Well, go stand in the corner!" Veneer ordered.

"Oh, yes!" Crimp obeyed. She scurried over to the wall but couldn't find a corner. She looked around anxiously. Velvet and Veneer looked at each other, shaking their heads.

"OK, I cannot with her," Velvet said with a sigh.

"It's really too much," Veneer agreed.

Velvet headed towards Floyd's perfume bottle. "Well, time for a spritz . . ."

"No, please!" Floyd begged.

The siblings glared at him.

CHAPTER NINE

Floyd looked pale and drained. "I don't have any talent left to give," he croaked. "I mean, maybe a Christmas album or a one-off national anthem performance . . ."

Velvet glared at the poor Troll. "Oh, really? You don't? OK, that's fine. We'll just kiss our careers goodbye and focus our efforts on charity."

She didn't mean it. Grabbing the perfume bottle, she squeezed the bulb, giving herself a big spray of Troll talent. *SHHFFT!* Floyd groaned as the energy was sucked out of him. Velvet tested the results, opening her mouth to sing. She let loose an impressive cascade of notes. Satisfied, she smiled and aimed the bottle's nozzle at her brother's mouth. *SSSHHFFT!* "Your turn, Veneer."

Veneer coughed. "Ack! You're supposed to say it *before* you spray it, remember?"

Floyd knelt on the bottom of the bottle with his hands clasped together. "Please, guys. Stop sucking out all my talent!"

Velvet made a disgusted face. "What else do you want us to do to be famous? Work for it? I don't think so. We're so close to having everything we always knew we deserved to have." She noticed her brother looking doubtful. "Veneer? What's with your vibe and your face? Why do you have resting moody-vibe face?"

"I know we deserve to be famous just 'cause we want to," he said a little hesitantly. "But honestly, that dude looks rough." He nodded his perfect chin towards Floyd. "I doubt he'll last us through another warm-up, let alone an entire performance."

Velvet leaned over, studying Floyd. "You're right," she admitted. "But it's all going to change as soon as we have BroZone."

At the mention of the brothers' old band, Floyd perked up. "BroZone?"

Velvet smiled, her mouth curling into an ugly leer. "Yup! I wrote a letter, begging them to come and save you." She kissed her own shoulder. "I love me!"

"That's how John Dory knew where I was," Floyd said, realising.

"They're on their way to save you as we speak," Velvet gloated. "And once they get here, let's hope there's enough room in that bottle for all of you."

Horrified, Floyd cried, "No! You leave my brothers alone!"

Rolling her eyes, Velvet said, "Ugh. I'm exhausted by this drama. Do you wanna go buy a yacht?"

"Oh, good idea!" Veneer said, clapping his hands together. "Let's buy *matching* yachts!" They left the dressing room without another word.

"Can I come out of the corner yet?" Crimp asked timidly.

Floyd looked at her with pity in his big violet eyes. "Girl, you need a new job. I should be the saddest one in this room."

In Rhonda, the armadillo-shaped van, the rescue party was ready to hit the road.

"Operation Family Harmony is on and POPPIN'!" Branch declared, flipping through an old fan magazine featuring BroZone on its cover.

Poppy noticed that Branch was actually *smiling*. He saw her look at him and immediately wiped the smile off his face.

"What?" he asked.

"Oh, nothing," Poppy said with the tiniest hint of a grin on her face. "I just, well, if I didn't know any better, I'd almost say you were excited."

"It has nothing to do with my brothers," Branch claimed.

Before Poppy could reply, a familiar voice said, "All right, all right! Branch, Poppy and this random dude, on another musical adventure filled with heart, hilarity and happiness." Branch, Poppy and John Dory turned and saw Tiny Diamond perched on a booster seat, driving the van.

"Tiny!" Poppy said, surprised. "What are you doing here?"

"Well, Aunt Poppy," Tiny Diamond answered, "for your information, I am no longer a baby. I am a big boy now, and I'm on a man-sized rite of passage to learn lessons of life, courage and maybe love." He flashed them his winning smile.

"Aww!" Poppy gushed, instantly won over.

But John Dory wasn't convinced. "Uh, should we be letting a baby drive?"

"Not to worry, fellow grown-up," Tiny

Diamond assured him. "I have procured my learner's permit." He held up a picture that definitely wasn't him.

Poppy leaned over, squinting to read the name on the card. "Who is Adulty McManface?"

"Enough chit-chat," John Dory said. "Step on it, Adulty McManface!"

Tiny Diamond used an extension to press down the pedal, and Rhonda leaped forwards!

CHAPTER TEN

Branch got right down to business.

"OK, guys, we've got to find our brothers, and fast. But don't worry: ol' Branch has got it handled. All we have to do is follow the clues." Yanking aside a cloth on the wall of the van, he revealed an elaborate collage of photos from fan magazines with labels and strings connecting them.

"Wow!" Poppy said, studying the pictures. "Check out your old outfits! Puffy jackets, pukka shell necklaces, denim tuxedos? Branch, did your hair have frosted tips?"

"Yeah," Branch said with a shrug. "It was an era."

"Don't forget his perm," John Dory said, grinning.

"No way," Poppy said. "Pictures, or it didn't happen."

John Dory handed her a photo of Baby Branch with a huge head of curly hair.

"AHHHHH!" she squealed. "Look at you! You were so cute! I love it!"

"Oh, but we had to pull the plug when he tried to frost his perm," John Dory revealed.

"It was an era!" Branch repeated sharply.

"Tragic," John Dory said, shaking his head sadly.

Branch turned back to his collection of pictures on the wall, searching for clues and connections. "While you two are strolling down memory lane, I'll work on finding Spruce." He pursed his lips, thinking.

Speaking quietly, Poppy told John Dory, "I'm going to need copies of that perm pic. Wallet-sized." He nodded, smiling.

"Listen, baby brother," John Dory said, turning back to Branch. "We don't need your little board to find Spruce—"

"It's not little," Branch protested, gesturing towards his picture board with both hands.

"Because I've got this!" John Dory crowed. "Ha! Booyah!" He held up a postcard with a picture of the sun setting over a beautiful tropical island.

Branch took the postcard from him and read the back. "'Wish you were here.' That's it? It's not even signed!"

"It's definitely from Spruce," John Dory said confidently. "I mean, he's the only one I know who talks that way."

Branch flipped the card over in his hand, examining it. "There's no return address. It's blank. This could be from anywhere. We can't find Spruce with this."

Plucking the card out of his hand, Poppy cried, "Yeah, we can! All we have to do is find this sunset." Branch snatched it back.

John Dory smiled. "Liking the optimism,

Poppy Seed." He turned to his brother. "Branch, one word: keeper!"

Grumbling, Branch walked to the front of the van and stood next to Tiny Diamond. "Hey, man," he said, holding up the postcard. "Look at what they think is going to lead us to Spruce. A postcard! We're never going to find Spruce with just a postcard. I bet this sunset doesn't even exist." He looked through the windscreen and was stunned to see a sunset that matched the one on the postcard exactly, tropical island and all. "Oh, man." He sighed. "Of course." He called back to Poppy and John Dory, "Hey, guys. You're going to want to see this."

"Oh, hot dog!" Tiny Diamond exclaimed. He liked the look of the beautiful island in the sea.

Poppy and John Dory rushed to the front of the van to look. They high-fived.

"I *knew* we'd find it!" Poppy said triumphantly. "Spruce must be on that island!"

John Dory lifted Tiny Diamond out of the

driver's seat and took his place at the wheel.

"Whoa!" Tiny Diamond cried. "Easy there, goggles!"

"All right, y'all," John Dory said, grabbing the wheel. "Let's mobilise!"

"Yeah, pedal to the metal, baby!" Poppy yelled.

John Dory accelerated, steering the van straight towards the ocean and the island!

"What are you doing?" Branch asked, alarmed.

"Worry not, my friends," John Dory assured them. "Rhonda here is completely waterproof."

The van plunged off a cliff and into the ocean!

"AAAAAAAAH!" Branch, Poppy and Tiny Diamond screamed.

CHAPTER ELEVEN

On a desolate beach, Rhonda washed up out of the ocean on to the golden sand. After a long moment, the Trolls spilled out, soaking wet.

"Good ol' Rhonda," Branch spluttered, shaking water out of his hair. "Completely waterproof, eh?"

They got to their feet and trudged out of the sand and into the jungle, which was thick with green plants. Poppy and John Dory led the way, clearing a narrow trail with sticks. Branch and Tiny Diamond brought up the rear.

Seeing an opportunity to pose questions about BroZone, Poppy asked, "So, um, John Dory, who wrote that song 'Girl I Love Your Love Girl'?"

He gave her a satisfied smile. "*I* did."

"Cool," Poppy said, pushing aside another tree limb. "Who wrote, um, 'Girl You Break My Heart Girl'?"

He nodded proudly and pointed a thumb at his chest. "*I* did."

"*So* cool," Poppy said admiringly. "Who wrote 'Girl I Love Your Love Girl You Break My Heart Girl I Still Love You But I Seriously Think We Should Have a Talk About Our Relationship Girl?'"

"That was Branch," John Dory replied.

Poppy was amazed! "Shut. Up! That was my favourite BroZone song ever!" She hugged Branch proudly.

"Joking!" John Dory admitted. "Also me. Branch has never written a song."

"I was a baby!" Branch pointed out. "What did you want me to write about? Nappy rash?"

"OK, take it easy, Baby Branch," chuckled John Dory.

Branch fumed at being treated like a baby.

He looked like he was about to lose it, and Poppy noticed.

"Hey, what's wrong?" she asked, concerned.

"Nothing," Branch fibbed. "Super happy. This is our most fun mission yet. Yay," he said flatly.

As they continued through the jungle, Poppy said, "Branch, do you know how lucky you are? A brother is a friend who can never leave you. It's the strongest bond in the world. I would kill to have a sibling to sing with."

"Yeah, well, you can have mine," Branch said bitterly.

Frustrated with Branch's negative attitude, Poppy said, "OK, fine," and ran off to catch up with John Dory.

Branch realised he'd blown it. "Poppy, wait—" he said. But she was already gone. Angry with himself, Branch marched forwards as the trail began to slant upwards.

Tiny Diamond caught up with him and said sympathetically, "Grown-up stuff, am I right?"

The trail got steeper and steeper. The four searchers struggled to climb up through the jungle. They had to find branches and plants to grab on to so they could pull themselves up the slope. Ahead in the lead, John Dory called back to the others, "All right, y'all! We're getting close to something. I can feel it—" *WHOMP!* He slammed right into an enormous creature, who turned out to be . . . a rock-climbing instructor!

"Whoa, what do we got here!" the instructor said, surveying the four little Trolls. "Looks like I found some fellow rock climbers!" What the searchers had thought was a wild, remote jungle cliff was actually a rock-climbing wall at a fancy tropical resort!

"Hi!" Poppy said, a little out of breath. She gave him a small wave.

The instructor grinned. "Welcome to Vacay Island!" he announced cheerfully, "where every day is a vacay!"

CHAPTER TWELVE

On the other side of the climbing wall, Vacay Island was a laid-back resort. The easy-going residents of the island spent their time lounging, playing, relaxing and singing. Happy music accompanied all their activities. Some islanders gently bopped Beach Ball Birds back and forth. The Beach Ball Birds couldn't get enough of it. Other residents tossed flying discs back and forth. Many lay on deckchairs, while others paddled lazily around in a shallow stream.

The residents were much taller than the Trolls. Their bodies resembled water balloons covered in terry cloth with pipe-cleaner arms and legs sticking out. Most wore their hair long. Many of the male residents had long moustaches.

Someone handed Poppy a fruity drink. She sipped it through a curly straw. Delicious!

They made their way through the crowd of islanders, searching for Spruce. Suddenly Poppy pointed. "Hey! There he is!"

She recognised his purple hair, which was even longer than in his BroZone days. Wearing white cut-off shorts, a black-and-white flowered waistcoat and a necklace with a white shell, he was out on the water, parasailing on a green surfboard, using his long hair as a sail. While he skimmed over the waves, he sang a song about how calm and happy sailing made him feel.

"Um, I think?" Poppy said, not absolutely sure it was him. She pulled out Spruce's old fan magazine photo for comparison. "Heartthrob," she said. Though his tummy had gotten bigger, she could still tell it was definitely him. "Oh, yeah. I totally see it."

When he reached the shore, Spruce got off his surfboard and headed into a building with a lit-up sign that read "Bruce & Sons & One Daughter". The sign included a big microphone. The building seemed to be a place where customers could buy refreshments and listen to music.

"Quick!" Branch said. "We can't lose him!" He and the others followed Spruce into the building. Inside, they saw lots of tables and chairs with customers, a small stage, and an indoor pool.

"CANNONBALL!" a Vacay Islander shouted as he jumped into the pool. *SPLASH!*

Spruce walked around the deck of the pool taking customers' orders. He clearly worked at the cantina. He called to another employee, "Hey, Lenny! We're almost out of seaweed floats!"

"Thanks, boss," Lenny said cheerfully.

So Spruce didn't just work there. He was the *boss*.

Cupping his hands around his mouth, John

Dory called to him. When he reached his
brother, he opened his arms for a hug, but
Spruce just handed him a menu. Spruce also
handed menus to Branch, Poppy and Tiny
Diamond.

"Specials are on the back," he said. "Don't
order the clams. Don't ask why." He turned
towards the kitchen and called out an order.
"Fricassee squid and one jellyfish slider!" Clearly
busy, he rushed off towards another table.

"Spruce!" Branch called after him. "Wait!"

When he heard the name 'Spruce', he stopped
in his tracks and turned back to look at him.
"Oh, no," he sighed. "I knew this would happen
one day. Listen, I know you recognise me
from BroZone, and I'm happy to give you an
autograph or whatever, but can you please be
discreet about it?"

John Dory stepped forwards. "Spruce, it's us.
It's your brothers!"

Spruce stared at them a moment. Then his

face lit up. He ran right past John Dory to Branch. "Whoa, *whoa!* Ha! BRANCH?"

"What?" John Dory said, stunned to be passed by in favour of his baby brother.

Grinning, Spruce picked up Branch and threw him in the air.

"Whoa!" Branch objected. "No tossing! Too big to be tossed!"

Spruce caught Branch and set him down. "The last time I saw you, you were in nappies!"

"Nappies," Branch said unenthusiastically. It was *not* his favourite topic. "Right."

"Wet willy!" Spruce shouted. He stuck a finger in his mouth to get it good and wet, then tried to shove it in Branch's ear.

"Ugh, stop it!" Branch yelled. "That's disgusting. I am a grown-up!"

"Oh, *sorry*," Spruce said, laughing. "A wet *william.*" He made one more quick attempt to stick his finger in Branch's ear, but Branch dodged him.

Trying to sound casual, but bursting with excitement at meeting BroZone's heartthrob, Poppy said, "Hi, Spruce. I'm Poppy. Wow, it's like – it's so cool to meet you, or whatever." She found herself blanking out on things to say – a very unusual experience for her. Then it occurred to her that she could introduce the fourth member of their party. "This is Tiny Diamond—"

But when she looked around, Tiny Diamond was no longer standing next to her. She spotted him heading straight for a huge bowl of nachos.

"'Sup?" he said to Spruce. "Killer nachos you got here, by the way!" He dived right into the bowl and started chowing down.

John Dory decided it was time to reveal their plan. "OK, Spruce, we're here because—"

Spruce held up a hand to stop him. "Actually," he corrected, "no one's called me Spruce in years. I go by Bruce now." That explained the sign on the building.

"I'm sorry, did you say 'Bruce'?" John Dory asked, confused to hear his brother had changed his name.

"Yeah, I wanted to put the whole boy-band thing behind me now that I'm a dad," Bruce explained.

John Dory looked surprised. "Wait a minute – you're a father?"

"Yeah!" Bruce said, full of fatherly pride and joy. "I can't wait for you to meet everyone."

Right on cue, Bruce's wife walked up. She was a Vacay Islander, much taller than the Trolls. Her long hair looked like yarn.

"Hi, honey!" Bruce said, greeting her. He gestured towards Branch and John Dory. "These are my brothers! Unexpectedly."

His wife raised her eyebrows, visibly surprised. "Oh, hello there!"

"Hi!" Poppy said.

"Hello!" said John Dory.

"This is my wife and business partner,

Brandy," Bruce explained. "She is my soulmate. My very tall soulmate. But we make it work."

Bruce's tall kids popped in with lots of requests. "Daddy! Daddy!" the first one cried. "Can I have a cookie?"

"Becoming a dad was like a seismic shift in my brain," Bruce continued.

"Daddy!" another kid whined. "Bruce Junior bit me!"

"No biting!" Bruce said.

"Daddy!" a third kid interrupted. "I don't see how any government stands a chance!"

Shrugging, Bruce agreed. "You're not wrong, kid."

"I'm stuck in this ketchup bottle!" a fourth kid announced.

"OK, I'm gonna handle all of that," Bruce assured his kids. "Just give Daddy two seconds, OK? Love you." He turned back to his brothers and Poppy. "As a dad—"

Another son jumped into Bruce's arms.

"DADDY, DADDY, DADDY! Guess what? I have PINK EYE!"

The Trolls took a step back. None of them wanted pink eye. It was *very* contagious. Tiny Diamond burrowed deeper into his nachos, hoping maybe the cheese sauce would protect him.

CHAPTER THIRTEEN

John Dory made another attempt at explaining their plan to rescue Floyd. "Look, Spruce, let's cut to the chase. We're not here to catch up. We're here because we need to hit the Perfect Family Harmony."

"Oh, no," Bruce said, looking annoyed. "You're still going on about that?" He turned to a couple of cantina waiters. "Hey, get these guys their meals TO GO."

He started to walk away, but John Dory stopped him. "No, no, no. You don't understand. It's for Floyd. He's being held captive."

"What?" Bruce said, looking shocked. "Well, then, what are we waiting for? We need to . . ."

"Hit the Perfect Family Harmony," John Dory said.

". . . call the authorities," Bruce said at the same time. He stared at John Dory, totally confused. Why was his brother insisting on hitting the Perfect Family Harmony when Floyd was being held captive?

"Spruce," John Dory said, not used to his new name yet. "It has to be us. Floyd's being held captive in a *diamond* prison."

"Oh," Bruce said matter-of-factly. "Well, yeah, you need the Perfect Family Harmony for that."

"Exactly," John Dory said, glad he'd finally gotten through to his brother.

Bruce realised something. "Wait. But how? We've never even come close to pulling it off. You do remember our last show, don't you?"

John Dory looked confident. "If we practise, I *know* we'll be able to nail it. We have to." He climbed up on to the karaoke stage and held out his hand to Bruce.

"At my age?" Bruce said, looking doubtful.

"I really don't think—"

One of his kids piped up. "See, guys? I *told* you Dad wasn't in a band."

Narrowing his eyes, Bruce looked determined. "Oh, I was in a band," he said. "I was in *the* band. You ask your mother if I was in a band!"

Brandy remembered how much she liked BroZone. "Oh. He was in a band," she confirmed.

Seeing an opportunity, Poppy decided to give Bruce a little encouragement. "Prove it. Prove it," she started chanting. Bruce's kids all joined in, balling their fists and pumping their arms in time with the chant. "PROVE IT! PROVE IT!"

Bruce took up the challenge. "Oh, I'll prove it," he said confidently. "I'll prove it right now. He took a deep breath and let it out. Then he hopped up on to the stage and stood next to John Dory.

"Yes!" John Dory cheered. "Bring it on, brother!" They hugged.

Poppy looked expectantly at Branch, waiting for him to join his brothers onstage. But he just stood planted in place next to her with his arms crossed over his waistcoat.

"Branch, get up there!" Poppy said, motioning towards the stage. "Go sing with your brothers!"

Branch shook his head stubbornly. "I'll do it to save Floyd when I have to. But I'm not doing it right now just for funzies, after not being listened to all day."

Deciding to try a little reverse psychology, Poppy said, "Yeah, OK. You're probably right."

Surprised, Branch asked, "Wait, what'd you say?"

"I agree with you," Poppy stated simply. "I don't think you can handle it, so I think you shouldn't do it."

"I'm not *afraid* of getting up there," Branch insisted. "And I literally saved the world. I think I can handle singing a song."

Pumping her fists, Poppy chanted, "Prove it. Prove it."

Bruce's kids joined in. "PROVE IT! PROVE IT!"

"I'm not falling for that," Branch said.

They kept chanting, "PROVE IT! PROVE IT!"

Rolling his eyes, Branch finally gave in. "Fine. Let's get it over with."

"Woo!" Poppy cheered. "Yeah!"

Branch got up onstage and joined his brothers. Poppy quickly snapped a cassette into a big yellow boom box and punched the Play button.

CHAPTER FOURTEEN

As John Dory and Bruce sang and danced together, the music washed away any tension that had crackled between them. At first Branch just stood beside them, watching. He began to sing, but he was just going through the motions, still not into it. Then suddenly, he started to feel the old energy he'd felt in his earliest days with BroZone, before things had gone wrong. A smile of pure joy broke out across his face as he danced and sang with his two older brothers.

Watching along with a crowd of onlookers, Poppy cried, "I can't believe this is really happening!" She loved seeing Branch look so happy.

Branch hit every note and every dance move perfectly, thoroughly enjoying himself. He and his brothers pulled Poppy up to join them. Thrilled, she danced and sang alongside them, remembering every lyric. They finished to wild applause from the Vacay Islanders.

"We still got it!" John Dory enthused.

"Tell me that didn't feel good!" Bruce agreed.

"I can't believe I remembered every word and every step!" Branch said, amazed. Though he didn't say it out loud, he also couldn't believe how great it felt, dancing and singing with his brothers again, like they did way back when he was just a little Baby Branch.

Poppy couldn't stop grinning. "Looks like your band days aren't behind you."

Bruce turned to his tall wife. "Um, Brandy, my love? So, I know we have a lot going on here, but do you think it would be crazy if I were to—"

"Leave me here to manage the restaurant and all these kids so you can go on a musically charged rescue mission with your brothers?" she interrupted.

"Yeah," Bruce said. "That."

Brandy smiled, shaking her head. "It'd be crazy if you *didn't*. You'll never forgive yourself if you don't help your brother. You should leave now before you get pink eye."

Early the next morning in Mount Rageous, Velvet and Veneer's harried assistant, Crimp, woke up with the sun and immediately got to work tending to the pop duo's every need and whim. Ironing a shirt, she heard a voice squeak, "Ow!"

She realised Veneer was already wearing the shirt.

"You just burned me!" Veneer said accusingly.

"I'm sorry," Crimp said. "Maybe it would be easier if you took your shirt off?"

"Ugh," he grunted. "Don't be lazy."

A stage manager popped her head through the dressing room door. "Knock, knock, knock –

it's 'we're ready for you' o'clock!"

Velvet faked a super-sweet manner. "Look at you, making your job fun. Good for you! Just give us five minutes. We're still working on our routine. OK, doll?" She closed the door and muttered, "Loser." Then she picked up Floyd's bottle, planning to take in another spray of his Troll talent before the day's singing began.

"Whoa, whoa, whoa!" Floyd cried, holding his hands up against the inside of the diamond bottle. "Come on, it's just dress rehearsal. You don't need me for a dress rehearsal!"

Ignoring his protests, Velvet grabbed the golden spray bulb between her fingers and pointed the nozzle at her mouth, ready to spritz her vocal cords. Her brother spoke up. "Wait. Maybe he's got a point. Do we even need a dress rehearsal?"

"Obviously," Velvet said, making a face. "That's why we're getting *dressed.*"

"I'm just saying he doesn't look so great,"

Veneer pointed out. "He has, like, sad Troll face."

Velvet shrugged it off. "He's fine."

"And he's getting pale," Veneer added. "And not in a stunning Victorian way."

In his bottle, Floyd noticed that his hand was turning transparent. "Ahhh! That's not good!"

"Yikes," Velvet said, peering at the trapped Troll.

"What does that mean?" Veneer asked.

But Velvet wasn't overly concerned about Floyd's see-through hand and overall paleness. "Oh, he just needs some blush," she suggested. "Or is there a mini tanning bed we can jam into the bottle with him?"

Floyd held up his clear hand. "Don't you see what you're doing? You're literally sucking the life out of me!"

"I say that to Crimp every day," Velvet said, rolling her eyes.

The assistant sighed sadly.

CHAPTER FIFTEEN

Veneer paced the dressing room floor, clutching his head. "What are we going to do? We obviously can't even rely on the Troll to get us through this dress rehearsal, let alone the Rage Dome show!"

Looking annoyed, Velvet said, "How come I always have to come up with something?"

"Because you're the mean one!" Veneer told her.

"I'm not mean – *I'm ambitious*!"

Her brother got an idea. "Oh, wait – I know! We could *practise*."

Velvet looked at Veneer like he'd lost his mind. "I want to be famous, but I'm never going to work for it. Eww!" The very idea disgusted her.

"Come on," Veneer pleaded. "We used to

make up little dances together all the time. Remember?" He did a dance, calling out the steps. "Hip, hip, twist, flip!"

Velvet was not impressed. "Our dances *stank*. That's the whole point. How many fans do you think we can get making up stinky dances?"

"But at least we had fun," Veneer pointed out.

"Fun?" Velvet said in disbelief. She gestured towards the luxurious features of their dressing room – the beautiful furnishings, the latest gadgets, the designer outfits. "Do you want to lose all this?" Picking up Floyd's diamond prison, she said, "Maybe we should just try shaking the bottle." She shook it. Floyd ricocheted around inside, banging against the hard surface.

"Ow! Ouch! Ooh, my knee! My other knee!" he cried.

FSSHHT! FSSSHT! FSSHHT! Velvet kept squeezing the golden bulb, spraying herself with Troll talent. With each spray, Floyd winced and became more transparent. He was starting to lose colour from his feet up.

Velvet tested the results, opening her mouth to sing. An impressive cascade of notes poured out. "It worked!" she cried, delighted. "Maybe even well enough for a solo act. But that's not up to me. Is it, Ven?" she asked pointedly. Setting the bottle down in front of him, she swept out of the lavish dressing room.

Watching her go, Veneer sighed and picked up the bottle.

"I think maybe I should get a vote," Floyd said.

"It's nothing personal," Veneer assured him. "I just love my sister." He looked around the room full of extravagant items, including a model racing car and a statue of the siblings. "And all my fame. And money. And things I bought." He opened his mouth wide, sprayed his throat and followed his sister out of the room.

Floyd looked at his body, becoming more

see-through by the minute. "Well," he said philosophically. "I lived, I loved, I lost."

To the accompaniment of gentle ukulele music, he sang quietly to himself. He looked and saw that it was Crimp who was playing the ukulele. "Your ukulele skills are improving," he said.

"Thank you," she replied, sadly strumming the strings.

CHAPTER SIXTEEN

On an empty road that night, Bruce steered Rhonda, listening to Velvet and Veneer sing one of their pop hits on the radio. "My kids love these guys!" he said. "We're a total Veneer household."

"They're the ones who are holding Floyd prisoner," John Dory called from the back of the van.

Bruce looked shocked. "Wow, everyone's getting cancelled these days."

As the song ended, the DJ announced, "That's Velvet and Veneer hitting the number-one spot with their latest track. Don't miss their show tomorrow night at the Rage Dome, where they'll be receiving the Lifer Award!"

Branch joined John Dory and Poppy at the

back of the van, where they were studying his collection of photos and magazine covers on the wall. "Guys," he asked, concerned, "will Floyd even make it through that show at the Rage Dome? How are we going to find Clay and save Floyd before tomorrow night?"

"Don't worry," Poppy reassured him. "We're going to make it. We've been looking for clues to find Clay."

"Oh, I'm sorry – the clue board? You mean *my* clue board? That I made? We like the clue board now?" Branch said. He felt that Poppy and John Dory hadn't shown the proper appreciation of his clue board when he'd first let them see it.

Studying an old photo of Clay from his BroZone days, Poppy asked, "What is he wearing?"

Branch leaned in for a closer look at the picture. "Oh, those are just his . . ." Suddenly Branch got an idea about how they could

find Clay. "His Funderdrawers! Of course!"
Luckily, John Dory had kept a small collection
of BroZone items, including a glass case that
held the original Funderdrawers – a pair of
underpants with a lightning bolt on them.
Branch broke open the case and held them up.

"Bleh!" Poppy said, pinching her nose.

"John Dory," Branch said, "I'm not sure why
you saved these Funderdrawers. It's incredibly
disgusting, but I'm glad you did."

"What? They're memorabilia," his brother
explained. "But I will be good gosh-darned if I
know how they're going to help us find Clay."

Moments later, Branch was holding a long
stick out the window of the van, dangling the
Funderdrawers in front of Rhonda's nose.
Catching the scent, she charged ahead, zipping
down the road!

"Help us, Rhonda!" Branch shouted happily.
"She's got the scent!"

Tiny Diamond was driving. John Dory

pointed to the dashboard. "Hey, Tiny. You see that button?" A big button was labelled HUSTLE.

It was hard not to see such a big, colourful button. "Uh, yeah," Tiny Diamond said.

"That button right there?" John Dory asked, wanting to be sure Tiny Diamond knew which one he meant.

"You mean the button that has taken every fibre of my being not to press?" Tiny asked. "Yeah, I see it."

John Dory smiled. "Press it."

"Oh, heck, yeah!" Tiny Diamond yelled, slamming his little fist down on the button. "Let's HUSTLE!"

VROOOOM! Rhonda zoomed so fast, she took them into a different reality for a moment!

"Whoa," Branch said, waving his hand around and seeing a rainbow trail through the air behind it. "Look at that!"

When Rhonda popped back into the reality

they were all familiar with, Tiny Diamond said, "I don't know about you guys, but I saw things no Tiny has ever seen before!"

Tracking Clay's scent, Rhonda pulled into an abandoned car park and rolled to a stop. It was dark and spooky. The only light came from Rhonda's eyes.

One at a time, the rescue team members stepped out into the empty lot. "Are we sure this is where Clay lives?" Branch asked, looking around. There were no signs of life anywhere.

"Are we *sure?*" Tiny Diamond repeated. "Our GPS is an armadillo bus sniffing an old pair of Funderdrawers. So, no. We're not sure."

Bruce felt the purple hair rising on the back of his neck. "I think this is the place from every true-crime podcast I've ever listened to." He looked around nervously, wondering what might pop out of the darkness.

They crept forwards cautiously, looking and listening for signs of life. Where could Clay possibly be in this creepy place?

Something scurried across a log. A pair of bright eyes blinked in the darkness. Someone seemed to be watching them . . .

"HALT! WHO GOES THERE!"

CHAPTER SEVENTEEN

Bright lights flashed on, revealing the source of the booming voice: A GIANT CLOWN HEAD!

"AAAAAHHHH!" they all screamed. Tiny Diamond burrowed into Bruce's purple hair to hide.

"Who DARES trespass on these sacred grounds?" the clown head challenged in its eerie voice. With its green face, orange hair, black eyebrows, staring eyes and gaping mouth, the clown looked terrifying. Thick smoke rose around it. As the clown head spoke, its teeth moved around in its mouth unnaturally.

Branch slowly took a step towards the clown head. "Branch, what are you *doing*?" John Dory hissed.

Branch kept walking until he was standing

right in front of the terrifying face lit against the dark night sky. "Listen," he said, looking up into the clown head's big eyes. "We don't want any clown-related trouble, OK? We're just here looking for our brother, Clay."

"Wait a second," the clown head said, its voice sounding less ominous. "You're TROLLS?"

"Uh, yeah," Branch said. "So what? You're a clown! Just the HEAD of a clown!"

What appeared to be a coloured golf ball rolled out of the clown's mouth and down its long, pink tongue. The rescuers huddled together, bracing themselves for an attack. But then the golf ball unrolled itself, opening up into . . . a Troll!

She was pink, with long, curling strands of yellow-blond hair rising into the air. She wore a white knitted one-piece leotard with gold trim and a red star on the tummy, pink-and-red leg warmers and a green cape that looked like it was cut from a putting green. Under each eye she sported a swathe of yellow glitter. Her eyes sparkled with interest and excitement.

"Oh my gosh! Hello!" she said, talking with incredible speed and energy. "My name is Viva! Woo! It is so fantast-a-mazing to see other Trolls!" She bounced from one Troll to the next, giving each a hug and an intensely warm look. "Hi! So, 'fantast-a-mazing' is my own personal word. It means, um, fantastic and amazing! I used to say 'a-mastic', but then I was like, bleh, that's not as good."

"Fantast-a-mawesome!" Poppy said, impressed by someone who had their own personal word.

"That's different, but that works too!" Viva said, nodding her approval. "Way to make it your own!"

The five friends were slightly stunned by the torrent of words that came tumbling out of Viva. It was a lot to take in, even for Poppy, who enjoyed high-energy communication. A thought occurred to her. "Is this how people feel when they meet me?" she whispered to Branch.

"Yes," he answered without hesitation.

Viva sensed that she might be coming on just a tad strong. "Am I being a lot?" she asked. "Sometimes I can be a lot."

Branch tried to bring the conversation around to their search for Clay. "I'm not sure if we're in the right place—" he started to say.

"Of *course* you're in the right place!" Viva interrupted. "Any Troll is welcome here with us." She turned to face the clown head, cupped her hands around her mouth, and called, "OK, Putt-Putt Trolls! Lights on for our new friends!"

KERCHUNK! Bright floodlights snapped on, revealing that they were standing in a long-abandoned mini-golf course called Hole 'N' Fun. The Hole 'N' Fun sign featured a Bergen in golf attire swinging a golf club, so Branch figured it must have originally been built by and for the Bergens. Sometimes mini-golf courses were called putt-putt golf courses, since players only putted the ball. The Trolls who lived there had taken to calling themselves Putt-Putt Trolls.

The clown's head was one hole on the course. The idea was to hit a golf ball up the clown's tongue, past the moving teeth, and into the mouth. Other fantastical holes included a dinosaur, a giant cheeseburger, a pig, an octopus, a huge hot dog and a big upside-down melting ice-cream cone. The visiting Trolls were awed by the sight of the incredible golf course.

"Oh my gosh, are you guys hungry?" Viva asked. "Are you thirsty?"

"Yes!" Tiny Diamond answered.

"You guys want French fries?" Viva suggested. "I'm seeing French fries." Once again, she turned and called to her fellow Putt-Putt Trolls. "Hey, everybody, bring out the works!" She snapped her fingers.

Dozens of golf balls of every colour imaginable

rolled out of the hidden spaces in the course and revealed themselves as Trolls. Several came running with big milkshakes and gigantic orders of French fries.

"Milkshakes to celebrate!" Viva announced.

"Coming in hot!" warned a Putt-Putt Troll carrying a huge basket of French fries.

Viva sucked down a milkshake. *SHHHLLLURPPP!* "Whew!" she said. "That's better. Now I finally have some energy!"

Poppy realised her hair was suddenly arranged into two French plaits. "Did you just plait my hair?" she asked Viva, patting her freshly styled pink locks.

"You're welcome!" Viva said, grinning. "It looks so good!"

"I love it!" Poppy gushed.

Bruce pulled a French fry from the giant basket and popped it in his mouth. "Wow," he said, chewing. "These fries are amazing. They'd really go great with a burger."

All the Putt-Putt Trolls gasped and stared at Bruce, halting in their tracks. They went silent.

Branch, Poppy, Tiny Diamond, John Dory and Bruce looked around, wondering why their hosts were reacting so badly to the mere mention of a burger.

"What is happening?" Bruce asked.

"Yeah, we try not to use that word around here," Viva explained. "It's just that 'burger' sounds a little bit too much like, uh . . ." She lowered her voice to a whisper. ". . . *Bergens.*"

At the mention of the forbidden word, the Putt-Putt Trolls gasped again.

Then a voice said, "So we just call them . . ."

CHAPTER EIGHTEEN

". . . meat circles," Clay said, stepping through
the crowd of Putt-Putt Trolls, who parted to
let him pass. With his long light-green hair, he
wore a green knitted one-piece jumper and
yellow-and-white wristbands. His wide nose and
bright eyes were blue.

"*Clay?*" John Dory, Bruce and Branch all
said in unison.

"How you been?" Clay asked casually.
Gesturing towards them, he told the Putt-Putt
Trolls, "Everybody, these are my brothers!"

"Clay!" John Dory called out warmly.

Clay looked at John Dory. He didn't seem
thrilled to see his oldest brother. "John," he said
somewhat formally. John Dory felt hurt by
Clay's aloof manner.

Seeing Bruce, Clay showed much more enthusiasm. "Wait a minute. Is that Spruce? What do you know!"

"Actually," Bruce gently corrected, "I go by Bruce now."

"Bruce!" Clay said. "Oooh, someone got fancy."

"Look who's talking!" Bruce teased. "Is that a sweater onesie?"

Clay held up both hands in a "you got me" gesture. "What can I say? When you co-run a place—"

Viva put an arm around Clay's shoulder. "Yeah, I'm the face of the operation, and Mr Clay takes care of the boring stuff!"

"Guilty!" Clay admitted. He and Viva tapped elbows and laughed. Then Clay noticed the third brother in the search party. His eyes opened wide in surprise. "Whoa. *Baby Branch*?"

"It's Big Branch now," he said, not liking being called a baby. Then he remembered that no one actually called him Big Branch. "I mean, or just Branch. Branch is fine."

Clay walked over to Branch and took his face in his hands, which made Branch uncomfortable. All his years of hiding in his underground bunker had left him not used to other Trolls touching him, and he still felt that way now. He peeled Clay's hands off his cheeks.

"Yeah, so . . ." he said awkwardly. Wanting to change Clay's focus from himself to someone else, he decided to introduce Poppy. "Clay, this is Poppy."

Poppy had no such qualms about physical contact. She threw her arms around Clay for a hug. "Hi, Clay! So great to finally meet you. Can you do the rusty robot for me?"

Clay looked taken aback by Poppy's request. "Yeah, no. I don't do that any more, OK?"

Laughing nervously, Poppy said, "Right, kidding. Can you imagine? I wouldn't just ask you to do that after meeting you two seconds ago. Who would do that?"

Clay could see she was embarrassed. He explained, "It's just that Fun Boy Clay is dead. Serious Boy Clay only does the well-oiled robot." He struck a robotic dance pose. "And it is no fun."

"I mean," Poppy gently disagreed, "that's still pretty fun."

John Dory smiled. "Yeah, same old Clay."

But Clay resented being treated like the same boy he'd been all those years before. "That's not true!" he protested. "If I was still fun, would I have chosen the golf course's administration building as my bedroom?" He pointed past all the fun, wacky structures to a small, plain brick building.

"Oh, right," Poppy said. The building certainly did look like the least fun place to live on the course.

"Anyway," Clay said, eager to change the subject, "I can't believe you all are here." Then he realised someone was missing. "Wait, where's Floyd?"

"That's why we're here," Branch explained. "Floyd's been taken prisoner in Mount Rageous by superstar singers Velvet and Veneer . . ."

John Dory, Bruce and Poppy joined in: ". . . and the only thing powerful enough to free him is the Perfect Family Harmony."

Tiny Diamond looked confused. "OK, either they just made that up or I have not been paying attention." He popped another big French fry into his mouth.

"Oh, man," Clay moaned, wincing. "You're still stuck on the Perfect Family Harmony thing?"

"Clay, this is a matter of life and death," John Dory told him.

"Why haven't you just called the authorities?" Clay asked. Before they could answer him, one possibility occurred to him. "Oh, unless Floyd is being held in an impenetrable diamond prison."

"Yeah, that," John Dory said, pointing at him as if to say, *Bingo.*

"OK, well, this sounds like a very *serious* matter that you need my very *serious* help with," Clay said, wanting them all to clearly understand that he was through being Fun Boy. If he was going to re-join his BroZone brothers, he wanted it to be on his own terms. "I'm in," he said.

"Great," Branch said, relieved. "But we need to leave for Mount Rageous, like, now."

Viva looked appalled. "You can't leave now. You just got here! Come on, let me show you around." She grabbed Poppy's hand and started to run off, but then stopped when she noticed that Poppy's Hug Time bracelet was opening up like a blooming flower and changing colour to remind her that it was . . .

"HUG TIME!" all the Putt-Putt Trolls shouted, embracing each other happily.

Viva examined Poppy's glowing bracelet closely. "Oooh, so cute!" she squealed. "Where'd you get that Hug Time bracelet?"

"My dad gave it to me," Poppy said.

Cocking her head to the side, Viva said, "OK, this is so totally random, but I used to have one just like it. Can I see that?"

Poppy took off her bracelet and handed it to Viva, who put it on. "Wow," Poppy exclaimed, "it fits you perfectly!"

"Yeah," Viva said, staring at the bracelet. She went quiet – uncharacteristically quiet for such a lively, energetic person – thinking. Finally, she said, "I'm sorry. What did you say your name was again?"

"I'm Poppy."

"Poppy?" Viva said, studying her. She moved her face in close to Poppy's, carefully examining her eyes, her nose, her ears – all her features. "OK, um, another totally random, weird question, but is your dad King Peppy?"

"Uh, yeah," Poppy said, wondering what Viva's sudden curiosity was all about.

Viva threw her arms around Poppy, lifting her off the ground in a big hug. "You're . . . you're alive!"

Confused, Poppy affirmed, "I'm alive!"

"This is unbelievable!" Viva cried. "I never thought I'd see you again!"

"Again?"

Viva held Poppy at arm's length, smiling. "Poppy, it's me! Viva! I'm your sister!

CHAPTER NINETEEN

Poppy couldn't believe the words she was hearing. *A sister?* She'd *always* wanted a sister. And now Viva was saying she had one? And that she'd had one all along? This was incredible news! "My . . . my *what?*" Poppy stammered.

"Your sister!" Viva repeated, smiling a big, joyful smile.

"Whoa," Branch and John Dory muttered, amazed.

"Hey, man," Tiny Diamond asked no one in particular, "am I the only one without a long-lost sibling?" He snatched another French fry and chomped it down.

Poppy was stunned. "What do you mean we're sisters? How could I have not known about you? I can't believe Dad didn't tell me I had a sister!"

"That is so Dad," Viva and Poppy said at the exact same time.

"Ahhh!" Poppy shouted, not knowing what to do with all the emotions she was feeling. "I can't . . . I can't believe this! I've always *dreamed* of having a sister! I was just saying this!" She called back to Branch, John Dory, Bruce and Tiny Diamond. "Wasn't I just saying this?" Poppy realised something. Turning back to Viva, she said, "This means we can plan each other's birthday parties—"

"Yeah!" Viva chimed in. "And weddings!"

"Yes!" Poppy agreed. "My best friend, Bridget, just had her wedding, and it went off without a hitch 'cause I was, like, the best maid of honour."

"You'd be the *best* maid of honour!" Viva cried.

"You and Bridget are going to LOVE each other," Poppy told her new-found sister.

"Oh my gosh, I'm going to love her!" Viva said. "I love what you love!"

"YES!" Poppy yelled.

"YES!" Viva yelled. Overcome with feelings, the two of them burst into singing about the joy of being sisters. Together they danced all over the mini-golf course, ducking in and out of all the funny structures, like the dinosaur and the giant cheesy meat circle. Grabbing a club, Viva whacked a ball and got a hole in one, setting off an eruption of sweets.

Inspired by Viva's example, Clay grabbed his siblings and started singing about the joys of being brothers. They followed Poppy and Viva as they danced their way through Skee-Ball lanes, a bubblegum machine, a soda machine, a record player and a pinball machine. They ended up at a concession stand, gorging on ice cream and hot dogs.

Viva led Poppy into the giant upside-down ice-cream cone hole on the mini golf course.

She'd made it into her cosy, colourful home. Once they'd settled in and got comfy, Viva told Poppy the story of how they'd come to be separated from each other for so many years.

"I used to live at the Troll Tree," Viva began, referring to the big tree all the Trolls had lived in peacefully before the Bergens thought that eating Trolls was the only thing that could make them happy. "I was there when you were born. You were SO cute! Kinda like you are now, only teensier and weensier, and—" Her eyes lit upon some strings and a bowl of sweets. "Oh! Do you want to make candy necklaces that we never finish because we eat all the candy?"

"Obviously!" Poppy said, enthusiastically jumping on board with Viva's plan. They both grabbed strings and started looping them through colourful sweets shaped like doughnuts. But Poppy still wanted to hear more about their history. "Veev, I'm going to need you to focus here and tell me everything. Why am I only just learning about you now? What happened?"

Viva picked up a sweet dispenser with a duck-billed mouth. She made its mouth move, speaking for it in a silly voice. "We got accidentally separated and I've lived here ever since. The end. Want to do candy toe rings next, after the necklaces?"

But Poppy still wanted more details. "Uh, accidentally separated?"

At the same time, Clay was telling his own version of how Viva and Poppy got separated to Branch, John Dory, Bruce and Tiny Diamond. "Viva doesn't like to talk about it," he explained. "It's too painful for her. But she's been here ever since the night of the great Bergen attack."

In the ice-cream cone structure, Poppy gently placed her hand on her big sister's shoulder. "Viva, are you talking about the night the Trolls escaped from Bergen Town?"

Viva visibly winced at the mention of Bergens. But she tried to sound casual as she answered,

"Oh, yeah. Yeah, I guess it was that night." She threaded more sweets on to the necklace she was making. Her hands shook a little.

Clay was telling his brothers and Tiny Diamond, "Not everyone made it out of that tree. Some of them got trapped by Bergens. They were *this* close to getting eaten, until Viva and some of the other Trolls fought them off. But by then, the tunnels had collapsed and they were cut off from the rest."

By coincidence, at the very same moment, King Peppy was lying on a couch back in Trolls Village, unburdening himself of his guilty memories.

"I kept screaming, 'No Troll left behind!' But when I went back in, the tunnels had collapsed. That's when I found Viva's Hug Time bracelet."

Back at the mini-golf course, Clay continued the story. Branch, John Dory, Bruce and Tiny Diamond listened closely to him, caught up in his tale.

"Viva found this old, abandoned Bergen golf course and transformed it into a Trolls utopia," said Clay. "We've formed this little sanctuary of survivors. I added fire exits. She added her heart and soul."

Viva was telling Poppy, "I've thought so many times about leaving to look for you and Dad." She held up a framed photo of herself, baby Poppy and their dad. "But it's not safe out there."

Still on the couch in Trolls Village, King Peppy said, "I know I should have told Poppy, but, well, my heart was broken. I felt like a failure. Not just as a king, but as a father. I feel so guilty. What do you think I should do?"

Sitting in a therapist's chair, Mr Dinkles said

in a deep voice, "I'm afraid that's our time for today."

"But I just revealed a major trauma!" King Peppy protested.

"Mew!" Mr Dinkles said, reverting to his little high-pitched squeak.

At the mini-golf course, Poppy told Viva, "OK, obviously this is a lot, and you should be able to open up about this at your own pace, but we'll have plenty of time to work through this on the way to Mount Rageous!" She took her big sister's hand and started out the door of the ice-cream cone structure, but Viva stopped dead in her tracks.

"Whoa! I am not going to Mount Rageous," she said firmly. "And neither are you, silly! You're never going to leave again."

CHAPTER TWENTY

Viva dashed out of her ice-cream cone home.

"Wait," Poppy called after her. "What was that last thing you said?"

After Clay finished his tale of the two separated sisters, he stood up and dusted himself off. "OK, guys," he told his brothers and Tiny Diamond. "If we're going to save Floyd, we need to get going."

"Yeah, hear you loud and clear, brother," John Dory agreed. "I'll go get Rhonda revved up."

"I'd also like to volunteer to keep track of our expenses," Clay offered.

Bruce smiled. "Yeah, I don't think you'll get any pushback on that front."

"I'll go get Poppy," Branch said, starting off. Clay grabbed his arm, stopping him. "Wait, hang on," Clay said. "There's no way Viva's going to let her go."

"What?" Branch asked, confused. "What are you talking about?"

Clay pointed to a barbed-wire fence around the mini-golf course. "Like I said, Viva's got some stuff going on, man. If we don't want to get trapped, we should sneak out now."

Too late.

THUD! The gate in the fence slammed down to the ground, locking them all inside the course. Following Viva's orders, a Putt-Putt Troll had yanked a rusty brown chain to close the gate. Rhonda was left alone outside the fence.

Clay spotted Viva standing nearby with her arms crossed. "Hey, Viva!" he said, trying to pretend he hadn't just been talking about her behind her back. "What's up, girl?"

Poppy ran over to her newfound sister. "Viva, what are you doing?"

"Basically, you're not leaving here, no matter

what, because it's just not safe out there," Viva said. "You're welcome."

John Dory walked over to Viva. "It's not safe out there for *Floyd!* That's why we've got to go. We have to save him!"

"Wait," Poppy said, getting an idea. "Is this about the Bergens? Because they stopped trying to eat us. That's all in the past!"

Viva looked sceptical. "Yeah, right. That's hilarious, Poppy. I'm laughing really hard."

"I'm serious, Viva," Poppy assured her. "Bridget, my best friend I was telling you about – she's a Bergen." Poppy pulled out a scrapbook and opened it to show pictures to Viva. "Look. Bridget and I do a million fun things together. We talk and we play games and we sing songs and we make up these *really bad* dances. Actually, it's a lot like what you and I have been doing. The world's a lot different than it used to be."

Viva looked at the pictures in the scrapbook, taking them in. But then she slowly shook her head. "You don't understand. I just got my sister back. I'm not going to lose her for anything." She handed the scrapbook back to Poppy, unsure what to think. The photos clearly showed Poppy with a Bergen. Still, the world outside the mini-golf course felt unsafe to her. How could she let her only sister go out into the dangerous world when they'd just been reunited after so many years apart?

"You don't have to go!" Viva insisted. "We have everything you need right here!"

While they were talking, Clay sneaked over to the gate, unlocked the padlock and climbed up to the pull chain to open the gate. Viva realised what he'd done. "Clay?" she said, feeling betrayed.

"I'm sorry, Viva," Clay said. "But we have to leave. I don't want to lose my brother, either." He told his brothers, Tiny Diamond and Poppy, "GO! NOW!" He jumped down from his perch and ran out the gate with them.

Viva chased them right up to the gate. "No, no! Poppy, wait!" She realised she was on the threshold of the outside world and backed up, afraid. "Poppy, please!" she called. "I want you to stay!"

Poppy stopped running and turned to face her sister while the others boarded Rhonda. She hated leaving so soon after finding out she had a sister. But she'd promised Branch and his brothers that she'd help rescue Floyd. She couldn't go back on her promise. "Viva, I can't do that," she said. "But you can come with us! And I know you think it's risky, and maybe it is, but it'll be worth it. Family is always worth it."

"No, no, no," Viva told her. "I can't."

Heartbroken, Poppy watched as the gate closed. She leaned her scrapbook against it for Viva. Branch ran up behind her. "You were right, Branch," Poppy said. "Family is . . . complicated."

CHAPTER TWENTY-ONE

In Velvet and Veneer's Rage Dome dressing room, Floyd's diamond bottle sat on a shelf next to four empty bottles labelled Heartthrob, Fun Boy, Old One and Baby. Floyd's bottle was now labelled Almost Dead One.

Velvet paced the room. "Still nothing?"

"No," Veneer answered, looking out the window.

"No sign of BroZone?" Velvet clarified.

"No," Veneer repeated.

"How about now?"

"Yes, they're here!"

"Really?"

"No," Veneer said. "Still no."

"OK, that one hurt," Velvet said accusingly.

From her work corner, Crimp asked, "Oh, by

the way, you know that thing you asked me for?"

"Space from you?" Velvet said nastily.

"No," Crimp said, confused. "You said you needed a way to make your smoothies even fruitier and drinkable onstage."

"You did?" Veneer asked his sister. It was the first he'd heard of this request.

Velvet shushed her brother. What she actually wanted was a way to inhale the Trolls talent onstage, but she figured Crimp would be more enthusiastic about coming up with a smoothie delivery system. "Yes," she told their assistant, "that is what I want. Go on."

"Well," Crimp said proudly, "I had an idea!" She pulled out a pair of black diamond shoulder pads. "Ta-da!"

Veneer looked unimpressed. "Crimp, honey, that's not an idea. Those are shoulder pads."

"He's right, Blimp," Velvet said, calling her by an insulting nickname. "You're embarrassing yourself and it's sad."

"I beg to differ," Crimp said, standing up for herself for once. She took one of the shoulder pads and opened the faceted compartment on top. "It's a high-powered vacuum. I finally put my master's degree in engineering to good use!" She started dropping fruit into the open chamber. "You just pop the grape or strawberry or blueberry or guava slice right in here, and it releases the fruit's essence through here." She snapped the lid closed. "Lightly tap this button when you're onstage."

Velvet snatched the shoulder pads from Crimp, shoved Floyd – still in the bottle – inside, and smashed the button repeatedly.

"Um, just tap lightly," Crimp repeated. "Like, once . . ."

The vacuum was much more powerful than the spray nozzle on the perfume bottle. Floyd's whole body was sucked upwards as his talent was drained. He groaned.

Velvet breathed in Floyd's Troll talent and

sang a dazzling run of notes.

"You said it was for smoothies!" Crimp cried. "If you use too much, you'll kill him. The plum I tested it on turned into a prune!"

Floyd looked terrified, trapped in the shoulder-pad chamber.

"I don't want to kill the little guy," Veneer told his sister. "They're kinda cute when they're up and about, banging on the walls, yelling to go home."

Angry, Velvet grabbed her brother's face. "Well, it's too late for that. You hear all those fans out there? They're screaming for me!" She swiftly corrected herself. "Us! You don't want to give up all the yachts and the bling and your illegal pet monkey, do you?"

Laughing nervously, Veneer said, "OK, I've made my peace with it!" He turned to their little assistant. "Great job, Cringe!" He'd never bothered to learn her real name.

Velvet stared at Crimp. "You're smarter than I

thought. Now I don't trust you."

"That's maybe not a rational response," Crimp said nervously. "Please don't put me in the cupboard."

But that's exactly what Velvet did. She shoved Crimp into the supply cupboard, slammed the door and locked it. Then she turned to Veneer. He was looking at Floyd, who had passed out. Velvet tried to wake him up. "Hello? Hello in there! Wake up! Wakey-wakey!" She took his bottle out of the shoulder pad and shook it. Floyd bounced around inside, but he didn't open his eyes.

The pop duo panicked.

"He's *dead?*" Veneer cried. "Oh, man. What have we done! What do we do!"

Velvet had an idea. She told her brother to stick Floyd in a glass ball. (She figured there was no reason to get rid of a perfectly good diamond perfume bottle.) Then she led the way into their private bathroom and lifted the lid off the toilet.

Veneer held up Floyd's ball and peered in at the unconscious Troll. "Goodbye, little guy," he said sadly. "My favourite thing about you was how famous you made me."

"Hurry up," Velvet urged.

But Floyd wasn't dead. He was just *pretending* to be dead, hoping for a chance to escape. When the siblings' attention was off him, Floyd opened his eyes and got to his feet. He threw all his body weight against the side of the ball, knocking it out of Veneer's hands. Running inside the ball, he rolled right out of the door.

Shocked, Velvet and Veneer just looked at each other for a moment.

"Wow," Veneer finally said. "I thought ghosts just floated away."

"Don't just stand there!" Velvet shouted. "Go get him!"

"Why does it have to be me?" Veneer whined.

"GO!"

CHAPTER TWENTY-TWO

Floyd rolled through the halls of the Rage Dome, pursued by Veneer. "Help!" the little Troll cried. "Help! Please, somebody?"

He spotted a janitor mopping the floor, but the custodian was wearing headphones and couldn't hear Floyd's cries for help.

"Help me, please!" Floyd shouted as loud as he could. "Hello!"

Veneer came sprinting down the hall, but when he hit the wet, freshly mopped patch, he slipped and fell, sliding right towards Floyd's glass ball. He stretched his arms out and grabbed it. Floyd pressed up against the inside of the transparent ball to talk to him.

"Please, Veneer," Floyd begged. "Just let me run past you. You can pretend you never saw me. It'll be our little secret."

"I can't," Veneer said, though he did feel sorry for the Troll.

"I know," Floyd said, defeated. "Velvet would kill you." But he decided not to give up just yet. He could see sympathy in Veneer's eyes. "But just because she's your sister doesn't mean you have to let her treat you like garbage."

"Doesn't it?" Veneer asked, as though this thought had never occurred to him before. His sister had treated him like garbage for so long, he thought that was just the way things were between younger brothers and older sisters.

Sensing he was getting through to Veneer, Floyd kept going. "No. Sibling or not, you deserve to be treated with kindness, and to be around people who would never try to change the you that you are."

"I just wanted to sing and dance with my big sister," Veneer said.

"Maybe it's time you learned to write your

own song," Floyd said.

Veneer considered this. But before he could answer, Velvet arrived. She snatched the glass ball out of her brother's hands.

"You got him!" she said happily. "Hey, I know I probably don't say this enough, but good job, bro. We make a really great team."

When Veneer saw his big sister smiling at him, his face lit up.

"Now come on," Velvet said, hurrying back into their dressing room. "We're about to go from superstars to *megastars*. We should also probably hire a new assistant, which feels like a *you* job."

Veneer followed her into the room. "Crimp!" he called. "Hire us a new assistant!"

Her muffled voice came through the locked cupboard door. "I'm on it!"

Tiny Diamond drove Rhonda towards Mount Rageous. John Dory pulled out a trunk containing their old costumes. He, Clay and Bruce squeezed into them. Branch stepped out from behind a changing screen wearing his signature nappy and pink goggles. He felt uncomfortable. The costumes took him right back to that awful day when his brothers had fought with each other and left him.

They tried singing one of their old songs, but John Dory soon cut them off. "Stop! Stop! Time-out. Let's take it again from the top. Spruce, I want some smoulder in those eyes. Clay, you're being too stiff. We need some sillier robot moves. Branch, maybe a smaller nappy."

"Or some clothes *not* from the toddler section," Branch grumbled.

"That's why I don't wear one of those," Tiny Diamond called back from the driver's seat. "It's a hard fit to pull off."

"Really great note, John Dory," Clay said sarcastically. "Super helpful. Thanks, thanks.

Now I have a creative note for you: STOP
BEING BOSSY!"

As his brothers began to bicker, Branch
quietly backed away, reverting to the role he'd
played all those years before, the role of the
youngest brother who got no say in matters.

"What!" John Dory objected. "I'm not being
bossy! I'm helping us to be better."

"You're forcing us to be perfect, just like you
always have," Clay argued. "So we can hit the
Perfect Family Harmony."

"Yeah, for *Floyd*," John Dory insisted.

"Is it?" Bruce asked pointedly. "Or is this all
just so you can tell people what to do again?"

"Wh-what?" John Dory asked, surprised by
this accusation.

Poppy stepped in with both hands up in a
calming gesture. "Guys, guys, this really isn't
helpful right now. Let's all maybe take five
and—"

Bruce got right in his brother's face. "This

isn't going to work if you keep being the same old John Dory."

"Yeah," Clay agreed. "We've all changed. Bruce settled down. Branch is slightly taller with zero glasses. And I'm not the guy who shoots milk out his nose and smiles through the burn!"

"Yup," Poppy said to herself, remembering past milk blasts through her nose. "Been there."

"But you're still just so, so . . ." Clay said, searching for the right word to describe his oldest brother.

"What? So *me*, right?" John Dory asked. "Well, I'm not *allowed* to change! I'm the oldest! I *had* to be the leader!"

Bruce shook his head. "You love bossing us around! Just admit it!"

John Dory couldn't believe what he was hearing. "Why do you think I left and moved to the middle of nowhere? So I didn't have to be in charge of anyone! Four little brothers is a lot of responsibility."

"Why do you think *I* left?" Bruce asked. "So no one would treat me like you did!"

"You know what, Spruce?" John Dory asked.

"It's BRUCE!" Clay yelled.

"Thank you, Clay!" Bruce said.

The argument seemed to have reached a peak. Branch finally spoke up. "Guys, we can't forget about Floyd."

His three brothers stopped fighting, snapped back to the reality of their goal by Branch's comment. "Branch is right," John Dory said. "We're here for Floyd. Let's just get this done and we can go our separate ways."

"Fine by me," Clay said.

"Same here," Bruce said.

But going their separate ways wasn't what Branch had thought was going to happen. Now that they'd found each other again, he'd assumed he and his brothers were going to stay together. That they'd all *want* to stay together.

"Wait, what?" he asked.

"What? The mission's the mission," John Dory said. Then he laughed. "You didn't think we'd all live together when this was over, did you? Singing songs and roasting marshmallows—"

Poppy gave Branch a worried look. She could tell John Dory's words were hurting him. And making him angry.

"Oh, I'm sorry, is that funny to you?" Branch snapped at John Dory. "That I might want us to actually be a family again?" He took a piece of paper out of his hair. "Tiny Diamond, pull over. Now."

CHAPTER TWENTY-THREE

Tiny Diamond slammed on the brakes.
ERRRRRNT! Rhonda came to an abrupt
stop, and they all were thrown forwards. They
stumbled to their feet.

"Don't be a baby, Branch," Bruce said,
annoyed that his little brother had stopped the
van and made them all fall over.

Branch angrily confronted Bruce and Clay.
"You're mad at John Dory, but you guys do the
exact same thing to me. You all still treat me
like the baby of the family. But guess what? I
stopped being a baby the day you guys walked
out on me. Then Grandma got eaten and there
was no one else to take care of me. So I grew
up! And this time, I'm walking out on you." He
crumpled up the piece of paper he'd taken out

of his hair, threw it on the ground and stomped out of the van without looking back.

Poppy picked up the crumpled paper and smoothed it out. "This is Branch's underground bunker," she said. Then she realised something. "He built it for *you guys*."

"I didn't know," John Dory said.

"I guess you never asked," Poppy said, going after Branch.

The older brothers watched her leave. Then Clay said, "Wait, Grandma got eaten?"

Outside, Poppy hurried to catch up with Branch. "Branch, wait!" she called after him. "Branch!" He kept on walking without looking back at her. "Where are you going?"

"To save Floyd," Branch answered over his shoulder. "Alone. I didn't need them growing up, and I don't need them now."

Poppy finally reached his side.

"What are you doing?" Branch asked, puzzled.

"What do you mean?" Poppy asked. "I'm coming with you."

"Why bother?" Branch asked bitterly. "Aren't you going to leave me eventually anyway? Everyone else does."

Grabbing his hand, Poppy said, "Branch, stop. I have been by your side from the moment we met. And you've been by mine. So let's give each other some credit here."

Branch realised he'd let his feelings about his brothers get confused with his feelings about Poppy. "Right. I'm sorry," he said. "Thank you."

"You're welcome," Poppy said, giving his hand a squeeze. "And I'm not going anywhere. Unless it's with you. To save Floyd." Branch smiled, and Poppy smiled back.

Tiny Diamond pedalled up beside them on a four-wheeled bike with high handlebars.

"Tiny!" Poppy cried, delighted to see him. "You're coming too?"

"What can I say?" Tiny said, shrugging his silver shoulders. "I was moved by Branch's speech and his sad, sad drawing. Now let's roll!"

Branch and Poppy climbed aboard, and the three Trolls started pedalling towards the glittering metropolis of Mount Rageous.

That evening, Bridget and Gristle were enjoying their honeymoon, rolling down the road on a colourful motorcycle. Bridget, who was driving, came to a sudden stop.

"Wait!" she said. "Do you smell—"

"FRENCH FRIES!" Gristle and Bridget cried at the same time. They were right in front of the old Hole 'N' Fun mini-golf course.

"Wow," Gristle exclaimed, looking up at the sign. "This place hasn't changed since I was a kid!" Sniffing the air for French fries, the two Bergens rolled through the gate into the golf course.

"We've got Bergens," a Putt-Putt Troll whispered. "Code Red." All over the course, Putt-Putt Trolls rolled themselves up into golf balls to hide.

Bridget and Gristle spotted the big baskets of French fries left behind by the Trolls earlier that day, sitting in front of the clown head. "Jackpot!" Bridget said happily. But as she reached for the delicious fries . . . the clown head lit up! Hundreds of brightly coloured golf balls rolled out from their hiding places and surrounded the newlyweds.

"Are those golf balls?" Bridget asked. The balls unrolled themselves, erupting into an army of Putt-Putt Trolls. "Oh, good." Bridget was relieved. "They're just Trolls! Look how cute they are!"

Chanting "Putt-putt-putt-putt," the army attacked, using long, sticky fake hands to lasso the royal couple and tie them down.

"Ahhhh!" Gristle screamed. "What is happening!"

CHAPTER TWENTY-FOUR

Mount Rageous was a shining city with buildings that looked as though they'd been cut from rock crystal. Bright pinks and purples dominated the colour scheme. Everything was brightly lit twenty-four hours a day. Seen from afar, the metropolis looked like a giantess had dumped all her jewellery in a big pile and aimed glaring spotlights at the faceted gems.

It wasn't hard for Branch, Poppy and Tiny Diamond to find the Rage Dome, since it was one of the biggest – and most dazzling – buildings in a city full of big, dazzling buildings. Celebrity performers walked along the Rage Dome's red carpet, heading into Velvet and Veneer's award ceremony, while excited fans clamoured for autographs and photos.

"Security is really tight," Branch said, "so we're not going to be able to just walk right in."

"Which means we're scaling the walls," Poppy said, up for the adventure.

Tiny Diamond wasn't so sure. "We're doing *what?*"

Wearing transparent pink gummy gloves on their hands, Branch, Poppy and Tiny Diamond climbed up the outside of the Rage Dome. *THWOMP. THWOMP. THWOMP. THWOMP.*

Tiny Diamond didn't like the climb at all. "I'm tired!" he complained. "Carry me!"

"You have to walk on your own, Tiny," Poppy told him. "You have to be a big boy."

"But my feet hurt," he whined. "I don't wanna!"

At the top, Branch pulled out a wad of candyfloss he kept in his hair for emergencies and tossed it into an air vent to jam the whirling blades of a fan. Then they dived down into the vent shaft past the stuck blades.

Wearing a welder's mask, Poppy used a blowtorch (Branch wasn't the only one who could store stuff in his hair!) to knock out the power so they wouldn't have to worry about any more spinning fans.

"How do you know which wires to cut?" Branch asked, impressed.

"I don't," Poppy admitted. "I'm just blasting everything until something turns off!"

Branch, Poppy and Tiny Diamond crawled through the Rage Dome's air ducts, searching for Floyd. Looking down through a ceiling vent, they spotted him in Velvet and Veneer's dressing room, still trapped in the diamond perfume bottle.

"Look!" Poppy cried. "There he is! Come on!"

The three rescuers slid down a rope and landed on a table next to Floyd's bottle.

"Floyd," Branch said.

Looking sickly, Floyd lit up when he saw his little brother. "Branch! Is it really you?"

"Yeah," Branch said, smiling. "It's really me."

"Wow," Floyd said, drawing close to the inside wall of his diamond prison. "You've really grown into that old *waistcoat* of mine. You're a real man now."

That was exactly what Branch had been wanting to hear. He hugged the cold, hard perfume bottle. "Finally, someone gets me," he said.

"I'm so happy to see you!" Floyd cried. "But you need to leave right now!"

"No, Floyd, it's OK," Poppy assured him. "We're here to rescue you."

Floyd shook his head. "This is a trap!" he warned. "Velvet and Veneer lured you here. You have to leave before they come back. Hurry!"

"No," Branch argued. "I'm not leaving here without you." Though he spoke firmly, he actually felt uncertain. On the one hand, he wanted to save Floyd. On the other hand, it was foolish to just walk right into a trap.

"Branch, please," Floyd pleaded. "Do it for me."

The dressing room's doorknob started to jiggle. They heard Velvet saying, "I told you BroZone would show up! My letter worked! I'm a genius!"

Dressed in their full performance costumes, Velvet and Veneer swept into the room. John Dory, Bruce and Clay were imprisoned in their faceted shoulder pads. Rhonda squirmed in Velvet's hands. Velvet paused a moment, cocking her head, listening. Had she heard something?

But Floyd sat alone in his bottle. Branch, Poppy and Tiny Diamond had slipped back up through the ceiling vent just in time.

CHAPTER TWENTY-FIVE

Peeking down through the grate, Branch saw his brothers caged in the crystal pads on Velvet's and Veneer's shoulders. "Oh no . . ." he said quietly.

Veneer was looking at Rhonda, still wriggling in Velvet's hand. "Oooh, what even *is* that thing?" he asked, grimacing. "Put it in the cupboard! Put it in the cupboard!" His sister unlocked the cupboard door, opened it and tossed Rhonda inside. Then she slammed the door closed. *WHAM!*

Crimp's muffled voice came through the door. "Hello!"

Grabbing Floyd's perfume bottle, she locked him into her shoulder pad. "Floyd!" Clay and John Dory cried. "Hey, bro, good to see you!" Clay added.

"Floyd, it's so good to see you!" John Dory said. "Listen, we would have been here sooner, but *somebody* – not naming names, but Spruce – couldn't stay on key!"

"Guys, please," Floyd said. The last thing he wanted at the moment was an argument between his brothers.

Clay looked exasperated. "John Dory, you're the one who parked in the spot marked *Reserved for BroZone*. That didn't seem at all fishy to you?"

"Oh, so it's my fault?" John Dory asked.

Veneer grinned. "Aww, they're even cute when they fight!" He tapped each shoulder-pad prison as if he were touching the Trolls' noses. "Boop, boop, boop, boop."

"What are you doing?" Floyd asked Veneer. "Come on, man, you're better than this."

"Why, thank you!" Veneer said, flattered.

Velvet told Floyd, "I don't see why you're so upset. At least we're putting your talent to good use. I mean, *you're welcome.*"

"What?" John Dory said. He couldn't believe the pop star expected them to be grateful to her for imprisoning them and drawing out their life force. "You're sick!"

Veneer waggled his finger disapprovingly. "You mispronounced 'Thank you for not letting our talents go to waste any more, Velvet and Veneer!'"

"Come on," Velvet said to her little brother. "They're waiting for us on the red carpet!"

As Velvet opened the dressing-room door, Branch, Poppy and Tiny Diamond heard screaming fans outside. The pop stars left with Floyd, John Dory, Clay and Bruce locked in their gem-like shoulder pads.

When they were gone, the three Trolls slid back down into the room and opened the cupboard door. Rhonda stood there, but Crimp was nowhere to be seen. Then Rhonda spat out Crimp. *SHPLOOT!*

"Um, hi!" Poppy said with a friendly little wave.

"Hi," the assistant said. "I'm Crimp." Her face crumpled. She'd done her absolute best for Velvet and Veneer, but in return they'd locked her in a cupboard and ordered her to find her own replacement.

"Oh, it looks like you need a hug," Poppy said. Crimp burst into tears and embraced Poppy.

"OK, now, whose sibling is this?" Tiny Diamond asked.

Tied up by the Putt-Putt Trolls, Bridget and Gristle found themselves being pulled towards the chomping teeth in the clown head's mouth. "Bergens! Bergens! Bergens!" the Putt-Putt Trolls chanted, waving torches in the air.

It looked to Gristle like the end. "Bridgie," he said, "loving you is the best thing that ever happened to me!"

Before Bridget could answer with a love declaration of her own, a voice shouted, "WAIT!"

The lights in the clown head went dark. Viva had shut them off. She jumped down next to Bridget. "Is this you?" she asked, holding Poppy's scrapbook open to a photo of Bridget and Poppy sneaking a bite of cake together before the wedding. They looked really happy.

"Hey, that's me and my best friend!" Bridget said.

"Yeah, Poppy," Viva said. "She's . . . she's my sister."

"You're Poppy's *sister*?" Bridget asked, her eyes widening in wonder. Poppy had never mentioned having a sister! "That makes us best friends too!"

Viva smiled. "She told me about your wedding. Congratulations."

"Thanks, girl," Bridget said.

Viva looked at the two Bergens, all tied up

on her orders. "I think I made a huge mistake."
She was thinking about her decision to stay
and hide instead of going with her sister to save
Floyd.

"It's fine," Gristle assured her. "We're not
going to press charges."

"I don't think that's what she means," Bridget
said.

"Yeah, no, that's not what I'm talking about,"
Viva said. Nonetheless, she quickly released
them. "So you're really not going to eat us?"

"No," Bridget said. "But I understand your
fear. If you want, I can open my mouth and
you can take tiny steps towards it, letting
yourself feel and breathe your way through the
anxiety. It's called systematic desensitisation."
She opened her mouth wide.

"Or," Viva suggested, "I let you go and you
promise not to eat us."

"Oh, that's fine too," Bridget said. They
smiled at each other.

CHAPTER TWENTY-SIX

All across Mount Rageous, Kid Ritz popped on to giant screens, reporting live from the Rage Dome. "All right, Rageons! Now is the moment you've all been waiting for! Everyone put your hands up for this year's Lifer Award recipients, Velvet and Veneer!"

As the mob of fans cheered, whistled, and clapped, Velvet and Veneer pulled up to the Rage Dome's red carpet in a luxurious red sports car, waving to their fans through the open sunroof.

"WE LOVE YOU, VELVET AND VENEER!" more than one fan screamed.

"Thank you!" Velvet said. "We love you, too!" She and Veneer dropped down into the car and closed the sunroof. "This is it!" Velvet told her brother, covering her shoulder pads with green-and-purple scarves. "Everything I've ever wanted! And it's just going to cost a couple of Trolls."

Once they both had their shoulder pads hidden, the pop stars climbed out of the car and started walking down the red carpet, signing autographs and posing for pictures along the way.

Suddenly the ground started to rumble and shake! Rhonda surfaced, bursting through the earth!

Branch jumped out of the van and pointed an accusing finger at the siblings. "Velvet and Veneer! Give me back my brothers!"

"Yeah!" Poppy said, joining him. "What he said!"

Velvet decided to go with complete denial. "You don't know what you're talking about, Trolls!"

"You're stealing BroZone's talent because you

have none of your own, you big PHONIES!"
Poppy said, pointing her own accusing finger at
them.

Crimp popped up out of the van. "They're
MEAN!" she shouted. "And I was their assistant,
so I KNOW!"

The fans, listening to this exchange, started
whispering to each other. Could what the little
Trolls and the papery mop with the glasses
were saying possibly be true?

"I guess they do know what they're talking
about," Velvet said to Veneer quietly. "OK, we
need to leave. Right now." The singers ran back
down the red carpet, jumped into the red sports
car and peeled out!

Branch and Poppy leaped back into Rhonda.
"Follow that luxury vehicle!" Poppy cried.

"On it, Poppy!" Tiny Diamond said. He
hit the gas, and they shot out into the streets
of Mount Rageous to chase after Velvet and
Veneer.

As they sped through the city, Velvet opened the sunroof and stood up. Cameras projected her image on to every screen in the city. She smiled and waved, while down in the car Veneer frantically reached across from the passenger seat to grab the steering wheel.

"What's up, Mount Rageous?" Velvet said. "You didn't think we were just going to give you a boring old stage show, did you?"

"That's what we explicitly bought tickets for!" a fan shouted.

Ignoring this sensible complaint, Velvet just went on. "We're taking this show ON THE ROAD!"

Cars full of screaming fans clustered around the red racing car, reaching towards Velvet and snapping photos.

Tiny Diamond still had to catch up with Velvet and Veneer. "I'm trying to get through," he told the others, "but they've got no respect for the blinker!" The blinker was Rhonda's eye, winking to indicate their desire to change lanes. The van swerved to the left and right, passing cars to catch up with the escaping pop stars.

Velvet lowered herself back down through the sunroof and punched a button on the car's dashboard. The roof folded back, clearing the way for a metal arm to rise out of the car, holding an entire round stage. Velvet and Veneer both hit the buttons on their shoulder pads and inhaled big whiffs of Trolls talent. The four brothers winced in pain.

"Floyd, why didn't you warn us about how uncomfortable that is?" John Dory asked.

The stage's spotlights turned on. After putting the car on autopilot, Velvet and Veneer rose up on to the stage, singing a medley of their greatest hits. Thanks to the stolen Trolls talent, they sounded terrific. The fans in the surrounding cars went wild.

Seeing that Rhonda was gaining on them, Velvet pressed a button with the sharp toe of one of her purple boots, kicking in the car's turbo boosters. *FWOOOM!* The car zoomed ahead, leaving Rhonda in its dust.

Branch spotted a ramp that curved right towards the spot Velvet and Veneer were speeding into as they rounded a bend in the road. To get to the ramp, Rhonda would have to cut across several lanes of thick traffic. Branch grabbed the steering wheel and yanked it to the left.

HONK! HONK! Furious drivers blasted their horns and swerved to avoid hitting Rhonda. There were several close calls, but the cute, determined van made it up the ramp . . . and soared off into the air!

CHAPTER TWENTY-SEVEN

As Rhonda rocketed towards Velvet and Veneer's moving stage, Tiny Diamond floated out of the driver's seat. Branch grabbed him and pulled him back down. "Hold her steady, Tiny!" Branch cried as he floated in mid-air.

Branch opened Rhonda's sunroof and saw Velvet and Veneer standing on their stage. He also saw Floyd imprisoned in Velvet's shoulder pad. Timing his jump exactly right, Branch leaped out of the sunroof and landed on Velvet's shoulder right next to Floyd.

"Branch!" Floyd called, amazed to see his little brother.

"Hang tight, Floyd!" Branch told him. "We'll get you guys out of here!"

But before Branch could even try to open the

shoulder pad, Velvet noticed him and swatted him away. "NO!" Branch screamed, flying towards Rhonda, who had barely managed to grab on to one of the stage's light towers with her stubby legs.

Branch held tight to Rhonda, but the little van lost her grip when the racing car swerved and went flying on to the road. The Trolls were tossed around like socks in a dryer! After a few somersaults, Rhonda regained her footing and zoomed down the avenue after Velvet and Veneer with all her passengers inside.

From the driver's seat, Tiny Diamond spotted a sign up ahead. "Uh, guys?" he asked anxiously. "What does 'end of the road' mean?"

Just ahead of them, barriers blocked the road. Tiny Diamond, Branch, Poppy and Crimp screamed! Velvet and Veneer launched themselves off the stage as their car slammed through the barriers, flew off the road and exploded into flames. *KABOOM!* Unfazed, the pop stars just kept singing, landing on one of their yachts, which was passing by on the river below.

Rhonda flew off the road and landed hard on the path that ran alongside the river. *WHUMP!* Dismayed, Poppy and Branch watched the yacht sail further and further away.

"Oh no," Branch moaned.

"What do we do?" Poppy asked.

Tiny Diamond, still at the wheel, turned and looked at them with a smile. "Let's hustle!" he said. He punched the Hustle button on the dashboard. Rhonda rattled, shook and shot up into the air in an explosion of light!

High above Mount Rageous, Rhonda shot out the Hustle Man, a mysterious figure who embodied the spirit of hustling. He grabbed Rhonda and flew towards the yacht.

"Hey, it's the Hustle Man!" Branch shouted.

Poppy pointed down to the yacht, where Velvet and Veneer were still singing. "Can you drop us down on that boat?" she asked.

"Abso-hustle-y!" the Hustle Man said agreeably. Sticking his hands straight out, he held Rhonda over the deck of the yacht.

Then he dropped her.

"Not literally!" Branch cried as they plummeted towards the boat.

Just as they were about to crash on to the yacht, sticky fake hands stretched out and caught Rhonda. The hands had been whipped out towards them by . . . Bridget and Gristle on their motorcycle!

"Bridget! Gristle!" Poppy cried joyfully, looking up out of Rhonda. "Perfect timing!"

"We would've been here sooner," Bridget explained, "but we had to make a pickup first." Viva stood, proudly revealing herself.

"VIVA!" Poppy shouted. She couldn't believe it! Her big sister had come to help rescue Floyd after all!

"You've got a really brave sister," Bridget told Poppy.

"Actually, I've got TWO really brave sisters!" Poppy said.

Viva jumped down into the van and faced her younger sister nervously. "Poppy, I'm really sorry. About before. I should've come with you. I was just—" She realised something. "Did you just plait my hair?"

Nodding and smiling, Poppy said, "I learned from the best. It's not perfect. It doesn't have to be. But we'll keep working on it, together."

"Together," Viva agreed. Her heart sang with joy.

Branch watched the two sisters hug, enjoying the moment. But then Tiny Diamond shouted, "Hold on!" Looking out of Rhonda's windscreen, he saw a truck with a ramp ahead of them. Bridget was racing the motorcycle right towards the ramp.

"Bridgie, what are you doing?!" Gristle cried.

"HANG ON TIGHT, GRISSY!" Bridget yelled.

"AAAAHHHHH!" Gristle screamed.

The motorcycle hit the ramp, zipped up it and soared off towards the yacht! "BEST HONEYMOON EVER!" Bridget whooped.

But the bike didn't land neatly on the deck of the boat. Its front wheel caught the very back of the yacht and teetered on the edge. Bridget tossed Rhonda on to the deck and everyone inside hurried out of the van – Tiny Diamond, Branch, Poppy, Viva and Crimp.

The motorcycle fell into the river. *SPLASH!*

CHAPTER TWENTY-EIGHT

Bubbles rose to the surface. Then Bridget and Gristle's heads popped up. They smiled. "Go get 'em, awesome sisters!" Bridget called as the yacht sailed on.

When she saw Branch, Poppy and Viva on the deck of the boat, Velvet wasn't dismayed. On the contrary, she was delighted! "More Trolls!" she exclaimed happily. "This will last us a lifetime!"

But when Velvet tried to catch Viva, the Putt-Putt Troll rolled to the side, pulled a couple of sticky fake hands out from under her cape and whipped them at Velvet's diamond shoulder pads, releasing the clear spheres holding John Dory and Bruce. The spheres landed on the deck.

"Are you guys all right?" Branch asked.

"Yeah, but she still has Clay and Floyd!" John Dory answered.

In their transparent spheres, John Dory and Bruce ran towards Velvet's feet. For a moment, she managed to stay upright, balancing on the balls, but then she fell, landing on her back. *WHAMP!*

Poppy, Branch and Viva rushed over to free Clay and Floyd. Break-dancing, Velvet spun on the ground. Veneer joined her, and together they flipped Poppy, Branch and Viva off Velvet's shoulder, sending them off to the back of the boat. Velvet thought they'd land in the river, but Viva whipped a toy spring out of her hair, and they used it to bounce back and fly through the sky! *SPROINNNNG!*

WHACK! The spring knocked into Clay's container, opening it and setting him free. As he fell, Poppy, Branch and Viva caught him in their arms. "Clay, are you OK?" Branch asked.

"I'm fine," Clay said, "but we need to get to

Floyd. He's running out of time!"

With only one Troll left in their shoulder pads, the pop duo decided to retreat. Still singing and dancing for the cameras, they climbed to the top of the yacht's tallest tower. Setting off fireworks, Velvet addressed the throngs of adoring fans watching. "All right!" she said. "Now who's ready for an encore?" She reached towards the button on her shoulder pad that would funnel out the last of Floyd's talent.

Watching from below, Bruce said, "Floyd will never make it. He's got nothing left!"

Veneer could also see that Floyd was practically transparent, almost completely drained of colour. "Encore? Sis, come on. This Troll won't even last you half a song. Let's just quit while we're on top!"

But Velvet refused to quit. "Just sing, you beautiful idiot!" She inhaled another burst of Floyd's Troll talent. Floyd's body lurched, and he groaned.

"Anyone have any ideas?" John Dory said desperately.

"Are you ready, Mount Rageous?" Velvet asked, preparing to unleash a volley of notes from her fortified throat.

Branch quickly huddled with Clay, Bruce and John Dory. "Guys, Poppy said something earlier and I realised she was right. We don't have to be perfect to be in harmony!"

"Here we go!" Velvet cried.

"We just need to be *together*," Branch told his brothers. They looked back at him. Their baby brother had grown up to become their leader, and they all knew it – even John Dory. "We'll follow your lead, Branch," he said.

At a control board, Crimp switched off Velvet's and Veneer's microphones. Then she grabbed another microphone, rushed it over to the Trolls brothers, and switched it on.

Branch took a deep breath, and started to sing.

CHAPTER TWENTY-NINE

Branch's voice sounded good, but it sounded even better when his brothers joined in. Angry and confused, Velvet glared at them. But they just kept singing. Working the controls, Crimp swung the cameras around to focus on BroZone.

The brothers added dance steps to their song. Poppy and Viva joined in. The crowd started to really get into it, smiling and dancing. The big screens around Velvet and Veneer showed nothing but the Trolls' performance. And it was smooth!

The onlookers went crazy for BroZone! As Velvet started to panic, Bridget and Gristle pulled themselves up on to the deck of the yacht, dripping wet. They watched the Trolls singing and dancing, amazed by their skill.

A force field of magical power started to glow around BroZone. Noticing, they grinned at each other. Their music was working!

Floyd's container started to glow too. Pulled out of Velvet's shoulder pad by the force of the brothers' singing, it rose into the air. Velvet desperately tried to pull it back down, but the energy of BroZone's music was much too strong to resist. The moving container yanked Velvet across the top of the tower and almost over the edge. Veneer grabbed his sister and hauled her back just in time.

Inside his bejewelled prison, Floyd regained just enough strength to add his singing voice to his brothers'. The diamond bottle began to shiver, shake and . . .

. . . explode! *FWOOOOOM!*

A blast of magical, musical energy burst out of the shattered diamond bottle, spreading across Mount Rageous. BroZone had hit the

Perfect Family Harmony!

The force of the explosion rocked the yacht's tower, sending Velvet and Veneer tumbling into the river and Floyd falling into Branch's arms. His eyes were closed. The Trolls huddled around him, worried.

"Floyd . . ." Branch said.

"Come on, man, wake up," Bruce urged. "Wake up, Floyd!"

"We need you, brother," John Dory said.

"Oh no . . ." Clay said.

Branch bent down close to Floyd's ear. "I built the hideout, Floyd," he said softly. "Just like in the plan I drew. Well, except for the ten-storey waterslide."

Floyd opened his eyes. "But how will we shower?" he asked.

His colour returned! The Trolls cheered and hugged. Around them, the crowd went wild.

The yacht came to a stop, wedged diagonally across a narrow passage in the river. Velvet climbed out of the water, turned the camera on herself and tried to sing.

She sounded awful.

The crowd gasped. "Hey, what happened to your voice?" a fan shouted.

Veneer decided it was time to come clean. "OK, fine," he said. "Listen up, Mount Rageons. We are FRAUDS! And we've been literally torturing little Trolls!"

The fans were horrified. One yelled, "My illusion of celebrity has been shattered!"

Crimp stepped in front of the pop duo. "It's true," she confirmed. "And they're mean. Not ambitious, but just plain MEAN!"

"Don't listen to them!" Velvet pleaded. "They're lying!"

"Oh, give it up, sis," Veneer told her. He faced the cameras. "We just wanted to be famous. Honestly, my sister wanted to be famous, and truly, I was too afraid to stand up to her."

Disgusted by her brother's admission, Velvet

said, "It's like I don't even know who you are."

"Yeah, you do," Veneer said firmly. "And you asked me to change anyway. Which isn't OK, family or not." He snapped a pair of handcuffs on to her slender wrists. She held them up, asking, "Veneer, what have you done?" Then she admired the shiny cuffs, saying, "Oooh, are these real silver?"

Crimp snapped a pair of handcuffs on Veneer. "What are you doing?" he cried. "I had a change of heart!"

"Oh, yeah, totally," Crimp said. "You also engaged in Trolls-napping, Trolls-torture, fraud—"

"Fair enough," Veneer conceded. "Prison it is!"

As guards led the siblings away, the crowd cheered. Poppy watched them go, smiling. Branch came up beside her. "So," she asked him, "how are you feeling?"

"Happy," Branch said. "Grateful. Proud. A little nervous, and sorry that it's taken me this long to open up to you."

"Whoa! TMI! Boundaries, my man. That is a lot of feelings," she teased.

Branch rolled his eyes and laughed. Poppy grabbed his face and pulled him in for a great big kiss!

While he and Poppy were still hugging, Branch felt something at the top of his head and looked up. "Um, what just happened?"

"Oh, it's fine," Poppy assured him. "Viva just plaited your hair. It means she likes you."

Viva joined their hug. "It means I like you!"

Grinning, Poppy said, "We're going to have the best family reunion ever."

"And a big, long talk with Dad," Viva added.

Poppy shook her head, smiling. "King of secrets, that guy."

"What is his deal?" Viva wondered.

"Aww, he's going to be so happy to see you," Poppy told her.

CHAPTER THIRTY

They set back off to Vacay Island where a stage had been set up on the beach, and a massive crowd had gathered. They were waiting for a show to start.

"BroZone! BroZone! BroZone!" they chanted.

Backstage, Branch scribbled lyrics on a sheet of paper for his brothers. "Bruce," he asked, "you doing your preshow exercises?"

"You bet!" Bruce said, wrestling with his kids instead of doing sit-ups. "Hey! No pulling out Daddy's chest hair! AHHHH!"

His wife, Brandy, reached down and took the kids off their father. "Break a leg, honey!" she told him.

Branch handed a lyric sheet to John Dory, who responded, "This new song you wrote is off the chain! I knew you had it in you. You are killing it, my man."

"I learned from the best," Branch said.

Clay walked up and put an arm around Branch's shoulders. "I'm sorry we didn't get to see you grow up. But I'm excited to get to hang out with you now."

"Yeah!" Branch agreed.

"Hey, you want to join my sad-book club?" Clay offered.

"Yeahhh, totally . . ." Branch said a little uncertainly. He spotted Floyd peeking through the curtains at the crowd of chanting fans. Walking up behind him, Branch asked, "What's the matter? You got the preshow jitters?"

Smiling wistfully, Floyd said, "I can't believe we almost missed out on all this."

"We shouldn't have let our differences break up our family," Clay put in, joining them.

John Dory walked up. "That's right. Because we don't have to be perfect to be in harmony.

We just have to be together."

Branch started to point out that *he* had told them exactly that, but he changed his mind. "You're right," he said. "Good point, bro."

Standing in a circle, the brothers each put a hand in. "On three," Branch said. "One . . . two . . . three!"

"IT'S BRO TIME!" they all said in unison, lifting their hands.

Over the loudspeaker, Crimp announced, "Ladies and gentlemen, you know 'em, you love 'em – give it up for the Trolls Kingdom's very own . . . BROZONE!" She opened the curtains, revealing the five brothers in sparkling new costumes. The crowd went wild!

In the front row, Poppy cheered along with them. Branch offered her his hand. "Poppy," he said. "I have a small proposal. Will you—"

"Join the band?" she interrupted, bursting with excitement. "Of COURSE I will! I thought you'd never ask!"

"You know me too well," Branch said, grinning. "Now get up here and sing with us!"

"AAAAHH!" she squealed, leaping on to the stage. She extended a hand to her sister in the front row. "Viva! Viva, get up here! We're in the band!"

"This is my dream life!" Viva cried, joining her and whipping out a pair of castanets.

The seven Trolls joyfully sang and danced together, and the audience absolutely loved it. The concert turned into an epic dance party. Fireworks exploded, lighting up the night sky.

Poppy turned to Branch. "I love you, Branch!"

"And I love you, Poppy!" Branch told her.

"Would it be so weird if I fainted?" Poppy said. "Oh, I'm gonna faint right now."

And she did. But Branch caught her. He would always be there to catch her when she fell, and she would do the same for him, no matter what.

The End